Gardens of the American South

John Wedda

Westover
Publishing Company

A Media General Publication

Dedication

To Bruce and Susan and all those of their generation
whose reverence for nature is its best hope.

Foreword

As we continue to scrawl our vulgar graffiti across
mountainside and meadow, we leave a tragic legacy for
future generations. We are destroying with wire, steel,
macadam, and cement the purifying green; replacing views
of land and sea with hard sell; blotting out star shine with
neon glare; erasing sun with smoke and smog. Yet there are
those who go on saying, "I love you" to the earth. They
speak in several tongues, the most beautiful of which is
gardening.

From the flat calm of the tidewater lands to the gentle roll of
the Piedmont—from the pitch and toss of the Blue Ridge to
the steep crestings of the Smokies—back down to the smooth
slope of the Mississippi and the hurricane torn bayous of the
Gulf Coast—and up again, up the long swell of Georgia—the
patterns of life change; the insects, the animals, the growths,
the tastes and styles change; architecture, sculpture, the
fences change from brick to stone to wood to iron—and the
earth changes, black, brown, yellow, gray, ochre, orange,
and red—but the people are the same. They show superficial
differences but their essentials remain constant despite their
various conditioning influences.

There are other constants:
Flowers and green growth are as beautiful to the poor as to
the rich and those in between
Water means as much to all
The breeze is as soft or as cool
The rain as wet
The sun as warm
The birdsongs as melodious
The stars as bright for those who would feel or see or hear
The pulse of the earth and the sea beats for all things, for all
things are of the earth and the sea.
Wind and bird and insect and beast and man spread seed,
plant, and foster life.

Nature, the total of life, is the real gardener. Man is only one of the tools of nature. Man calls himself "gardener" but is just an instrument of a higher force which makes the seasons, brings wind and rain, sun and cloud, and puts life into the seed.

The restorers of the land and forest, the cleaners of the air and water, the growers of gardens demonstrate again and again the vital need to cooperate with nature rather than attempt to control or dominate it.

The gardens of the American South are wonderfully varied. Where the air is moist and warm from the sea, live oaks, water oaks, pines, and even wire fences are draped with epiphytic fronds of Spanish moss. The moss hangs, almost indistinguishable from its host, until one takes a closer look. Inland and upland there is no trace of the moss.

Gardens large and small remain from the past. Most of these have been restored; the women of the garden clubs and historical societies are to be credited with these important accomplishments. Philanthropy and feelings of civic responsibility contribute to the development of additional places open to public viewing and enjoyment.

Increased travel, contact with, and knowledge of far places continue and broaden the internationalism which almost all gardens, new and old, reflect. Perhaps internationalism is the wrong word since flora and fauna recognize no artificial boundaries. The only boundaries respected by the creatures of nature are climate and soil characteristics which are hospitable or inhospitable.

Partly because gardeners hate to see anything die or be wasted, they exchange plants which they have thinned out. There is a generosity between gardeners which effectively serves to propagate their own successes.

The exchanges often result in new uses for old plants. A plant hitherto used in formal plantings may find a happy home in an informal garden and plants which have been traditional in informal gardens may become prized parts of formal beds.

All this is part of the creative art which is well served by both traditionalists and innovators. The traditionalists keep alive the successful expressions created by innovators of the past and current innovators, seeking new expressions, create the traditions of tomorrow.

Too many people view beautiful, large gardens and say, "It's all so lovely but I could never have anything like it. I don't have the time, the money, or the land to have anything so extensive." So saying, they then view only as spectators rather than as actual or potential participants.

It is not the intent of this book simply to provide a vicarious garden tour, pleasant as such might be. The history attached to many of the gardens shown is interesting and important but is incidental to the continuing relationship between man and nature the gardens reflect. It is the intent of this book to provide many people the opportunity to see a variety of approaches which have successfully been taken to enhance the appearance of city, town, and country lands. Hopefully, it will inspire some to do more with their private and public areas not yet covered by cement, macadam, or buildings . . . to benefit from this viewing of large and small gardens by seeing how others have solved landscaping or land use problems . . . by applying themselves to their own problems, finding new and better ways of expressing themselves through gardening, and by saving another little piece of the earth for today and tomorrow and tomorrow's tomorrow.

the Gardens

VIRGINIA

Mount Vernon Kitchen Garden
Mount Vernon, Virginia

After he made a pilgrimage to Mount Vernon, Andrew Jackson wrote down his impressions of his visit to what he described as, "the venerable dwelling of the patriarch of our liberties." He wrote, "A neat little flower garden, laid out and trimmed with the utmost exactness, ornamented with green and hot houses in which flourish the most beautiful of the tropical plants, affords a happy relief to the solemn impressions produced by a view of the antique structure it adjoins, and leads you insensibly into the most delightful reverie, in which you review in imagination the manner in which the greatest and the best of men, after the most busy and eventful life, retired into privacy and amused the evening of his days."

It is remarkable that Washington could have found the time to create and oversee the landscaping and the gardening of his estate on the Potomac. The entire project is typical of his thoroughness and creativity. He began, a few months after his marriage in 1759, by ordering books on gardening which he studied and used for inspiration and guidance. His experience in surveying had already given him an appreciation of order and symmetry of design. He respected tradition but, in his gardening, he was also an adventurous experimenter.

To either side of the forecourt and the bowling green run the shaded serpentine avenues outside of which are the two walled, shield-shaped gardens. Of the two, the Kitchen Garden is the older, having been laid out in 1760. Actually, though one is called the Kitchen Garden and the other the Flower Garden, each was planted as a kitchen and fruit garden with flowers. Vegetables were planted in beds of geometric design with edgings of herbs. Espaliered fruit trees and hedges accented the design plans. Both gardens began as rectangles but, after the Revolution, General Washington extended the west ends to form asymmetrical points at which he located the seed house in the Kitchen Garden and the garden retreat (often called the Schoolhouse) in the Flower Garden.

The equal importance of flowers and vegetables in the gardens is suggested in George Washington's diaries. Dated November 14, 1788, is this entry: "Mr. Wilming, the German Gentleman above mentioned . . . offered to engage a Gardener for me and to send him in a ship from Bremen . . . he is to be a compleat Kitchen Gardener with a competent knowledge of flowers and a Green House."

Miniature apple trees are espaliered to form a low fence around garden beds.

The exchanging of plants and slips so characteristic of gardeners was practiced by General Washington whose gardens were given great variety by gifts from his many admirers and friends. George Mason of nearby Gunston Hall sent plants of Persian jasmine, guelder rose, and cherry grafts. It was not a one-sided thing, however. In a note to his manager dated Philadelphia, March 22, 1795, the General wrote: "Tell the gardener, when he dresses the Artichokes, to put up a number of the slips, securely, for a Gentleman of my acquaintance; and let them be sent by the first vessel to this city."

All the plant materials grown in the Kitchen Garden today are mentioned in the diaries and correspondence of General Washington. However, the 18th century varieties of most of the fruits and vegetables are not now available and modern substitutes are cultivated in the 18th century manner.

Mount Vernon has been restored and is maintained by the Mount Vernon Ladies' Association whose members serve without remuneration. The organization was founded by Miss Ann Pamela Cunningham of South Carolina, and chartered by the State of Virginia. Two hundred thousand dollars was raised by public subscription and a two-hundred-acre tract, including the mansion, wharf, and all subsidiary outbuildings, was acquired in 1858. The property had been offered to the Government of the United States and to the Commonwealth of Virginia but each had refused to purchase. Miss Cunningham and the American people were the saviors of Mount Vernon.

Many of the household furnishings had been distributed to members of the Washington and Custis families or sold by executors after the death of Mrs. Washington. Year after year, by purchase or donation or bequest, the original furnishings are being returned to Mount Vernon. At the present time, most of the pieces on the first floor and all of those in the master's bedchamber are things which were owned by the Washingtons.

Since 1858, the tract has been enlarged to nearly five hundred acres, a size sufficient to insure the property against undesirable encroachments.

Where honey was gathered in the seventeenth century.

The kitchen-gardens are on two levels.

Woodlawn Plantation
Mount Vernon, Virginia

Close by Mount Vernon is Woodlawn Plantation, given by General Washington to his nephew and foster daughter, Lawrence Lewis and Eleanor Parke Custis Lewis. Nelly Lewis was the daughter of Martha Washington's son by her first marriage. Nelly's father died when she was three years old and she and her younger brother became wards of the Washingtons.

In his retirement the General needed a secretary and host to assist him in the proper entertainment of the throngs who came to visit Mount Vernon. In 1797, he invited Lawrence Lewis to perform these services. Lewis accepted the post and, within a year, entered into a contract of marriage with Nelly Custis. The General immediately took steps to provide for the young couple's future. He set aside 2000 acres of his Mount Vernon lands for their use, to be inherited at his death, and urged them to start building on the hill overlooking Mount Vernon and the Potomac. The house they built was designed by Dr. William Thornton, first architect of the U.S. Capitol.

The estate was purchased in 1948 by the Woodlawn Public Foundation from whom the National Trust for Historic Preservation took over the administration of the property in 1951. Title to the property was acquired by the Trust in 1957. The Garden Club of Virginia completed the restoration of the gardens in 1958.

Much of the reference material which guided the restorers was found in correspondence between Nelly and Elizabeth Gibson of Philadelphia. Exact locations and patterns of walls, beds, drive, and serpentine walks were determined by the relationships of old trees and shrubs and by careful cross-ditch digging.

The original pleasure garden was lost to Woodlawn when the Fort Belvoir housing development came into being. As a substitute for the lost flower garden a replacement has been created in the area that was the kitchen garden. On the premise that Nelly would have been strongly influenced by the Mount Vernon gardens, Woodlawn's replacement followed that basic pattern. It is framed in peach, cherry, and cedar. The balanced arrangement of the twin parterres is devoted to roses, a favorite of the Lewis family, and garnished with spring flowering bulbs and summer annuals. Taller focal points are crape myrtle and chaste trees. Borders of the long walk to the summer house bring changing color to three seasons. Coral honeysuckle climbs the colonnades at Mount Vernon and at Woodlawn scales the summer house gazebo.

That Nelly Lewis did follow the pattern devised by her foster father is demonstrated by the story she told of drawing for her children the design of the parterre in her garden. When she finished, her daughter Angela exclaimed, "Mama, it is a rose!" George Washington's pattern was that of a wild rose bloom.

It is not surprising that the gardens of the two estates were as closely related as were their owners. That both are maintained today is attributable to the lasting affection of the American people for their first President, George Washington.

Much of the original pleasure garden was lost to urbanization before restoration was accomplished.

Gunston Hall
Lorton, Virginia

Colonial Home and Gardens of George Mason, Author of the Virginia Declaration of Rights.

Gunston Hall, like its builder, is truly great: firm, solid and stately without being imposing; articulate but modest; handsome but not flamboyant; the simple facade clothes a rich interior.

George Mason was one of the illustrious company known as The Founding Fathers of our country. Among them, Mason was called the "Pen of the Revolution" for he was the author of the Fairfax Resolves, of the first Constitution of Virginia, and of the Virginia Declaration of Rights. Adopted by the House of Burgesses at Williamsburg on June 12, 1776, the Declaration was to become the chief basis of the Federal Bill of Rights, for the 1789 French Declaration of the Rights of Man, and, since then, of almost every written constitution of the countries which gained representative government in the 19th and 20th centuries, and of the Charter of the United Nations.

After the Revolution, Mason was a delegate to the Constitutional Convention of 1787 where he refused to sign the Constitution because it did not provide for the abolition of slavery nor sufficiently safeguard the rights of the individual. He saw his stand rewarded when part of his dream was realized with the adoption of the Bill of Rights. Within a year he died, having just enjoyed a last visit from his friend, Thomas Jefferson, who called him "the wisest man of his generation."

Today, Gunston Hall and its gardens are to be seen as restored by the Garden Club of Virginia and the National Society of the Colonial Dames of America. It is, under the terms of the donor's will, the property of the Commonwealth of Virginia and is under the custodianship of a Board of Regents chosen from the National Society of the Colonial Dames of America. The donor, Louis Hertle, had bought the estate in 1912 and spent large sums to bring the gardens back to their one-time splendor.

The great feature of Gunston is the unusual extent of the boxwood planting. The then British Foreign Minister, Lord Balfour, once said that the box was the finest he had seen anywhere, including England, with the possible exception of the Vatican. He later wrote that after visiting the Vatican he was convinced that the boxwood at Gunston was the tallest and best in the world.

A long entry road leads through laurel-rich woods, across open fields, past orchards and a rose-laden post and rail fence, through an avenue of great magnolias to the circular drive before the house.

The restoration meant the transformation of what had become a 20th century garden to one of 18th century character. This meant

It has been said that the boxwood green gardens at Gunston are the greatest in the world.

the removal of pools, fountains, figures, summer house, and all plant material not used in colonial gardens. After the elimination of everything unauthentic, the ornamental flower bed parterres were planted in dwarf box. Those nearer the residence house spring bulbs in a ground cover of periwinkle centered by topiaries of simple shape. In the farther parterres are irises, long-flowering phlox, summer annuals, and old roses. Tall cedars were used for accent and outline.

There is a lower parterre garden lying at the base of a sharp drop whose banks are covered with flowering quince. At the ends of the garden, on mound extensions of the upper level, stand a pair of Chinese Chippendale gazebos from whose shelter the garden may be viewed to best advantage. Beyond are the lower meadows, the Potomac, and the Maryland Hills.

The 18th century garden colors are augmented by tree and herbaceous peonies, perennials, hollies, locust, and fringe trees of crape myrtle. There is color for all seasons but the great glory of Gunston is its old boxwood which forms a letter "T." The crossbar of the "T" had suffered damage and large sections needed replacement. It was a difficult task first to find worthy specimens and, second, to convince their owners to part with them. The moving of such huge plants provided another set of problems. The job was done and there were ninety feet of boxwood seven to nine feet high and 14 to 18 feet wide which had a new home and the pride of Gunston was again intact. In April of 1954 the restored garden was presented to the Regents.

Appropriate to George Mason's feeling about slavery is the loyalty of the staff of black gardeners whose dedication was epitomized by the late Thurman Bushrod who was for many years the indefatigable head gardener at Gunston. His great service was honored at a special celebration on April 13, 1966. The bronze plaque which was unveiled reads: "In honor of Thurman Bushrod who for more than half a century

has, through his skill and devotion, maintained and enhanced the beauty of these gardens."

Thurman Bushrod died on December 18, 1967. The director of Gunston Hall wrote, "None of us, the past Regents, the present Regents, nor the staff can think of Gunston Hall without Thurman. He was more than our head gardener, more than a person to whom we all looked for guidance and advice about the gardens. He was an institution, and those who admired and respected him came from all parts of the United States and from foreign countries. His loss is not confined to those of us who were fortunate enough to have close association with him, but is a loss that will be felt by those who loved and admired fine gardens."

Ernest Bushrod, Thurman's younger brother, has succeeded to the head gardenership at Gunston and maintains a tradition important to it, to the Bushrod family, and to Mount Vernon where, during the years before acquisition and restoration, members of the Bushrod family went up from Gunston to take care of the gardens and guard against vandalism.

The recognition of Thurman Bushrod's services at Gunston might well have been directed to include the many other black gardeners without whose services the maintenance of most of the large gardens would be almost impossible today.

Of Gunston Hall Marian Buckley Cox, Regent from New York, said, "We must remember that all this beauty, all this invocation of the gracious American past is in memory of George Mason of Gunston Hall. Without him there would be no Bill of Rights in our Constitution, no Oath of Office of the President of the United States; and the citizens of Ohio, Indiana, Wisconsin, Michigan, and Illinois would be British subjects and under the Governor of Quebec, for it was George Mason's study of the Virginia Charters which saved this vast Northwest Territory to the Colonies and later to the United States of America."

Gunston Hall is as unpretentious as its builder,
George Mason.

Monticello
Charlottesville, Virginia

Thomas Jefferson, architect, landscapist, statesman, revolutionary, philosopher, founding father, and President of his country wrote: "I have often thought that if heaven had given me choice of my position and calling, it should have been on a rich spot of earth, well watered, and near a good market for the productions of the garden. No occupation is so delightful to me as the culture of the earth, and no culture comparable to that of the garden."

He also wrote: "The greatest service which can be rendered any country is, to add a useful plant to its culture; especially a bread grain . . . one service of this kind rendered to a nation, is worth more than all the victories of the most splendid pages of their history, and becomes a source of exalted pleasure to those who have been instrumental in it."

Monticello's site is atop the mountain chosen by Jefferson for the express purpose of creating on it his residence and gardens. Since he was a practical visionary who foresaw the degradation of cities and the dangers of over-urbanization it is understandable that Jefferson would choose a then-remote mountaintop looking out on the neighboring Blue Ridge mountains for his home.

At twenty-three, Jefferson began keeping a garden diary which he continued for 57 years until 1824, two years before his death. He was a keen student of landscape architecture and gardening which he felt were integral parts of structural architecture. He had a great regard for English gardening concepts but he did not stop with these. His studies of Greek philosophers and the early Christian educators imbued Jefferson with the belief that gardens were the ideal settings for the educational process. His studies revealed to him that from ancient Greece to the European Renaissance the most distinguished plans for education provided gardens whose most important functions were as outdoor studios,

The flag as it was when Jefferson served as President.

classrooms, and laboratories. When he designed the University of Virginia campus. Jefferson added to the old concept the philosophy of American democracy. He made the traditional cloister an open lawn bordered by colonnades which united faculty pavilions with student quarters; each with its individual gardens in which teachers and students could discourse in an atmosphere of natural harmony and growth.

Just before his death Jefferson was making plans for the establishment of a school of botany, along with a botanical garden, at the University.

Jefferson's reputation as a botanist led Benjamin Smith Barton to name a wild flower in his honor in 1792. It is the perennial herb with matted fibrous roots, sometimes called Rheumatism Root or Twinleaf, named *Jeffersonia Binata (diphylla)*. It was a plant Jefferson had introduced in the oval bed on the east side of the North Terrace. At the time of the Monticello restoration Jeffersonia had disappeared from that bed. Replacement plants were found at Snowden on the James River. Snowden was a plantation once owned by the Jefferson family.

As with so many places important to American history, Monticello's gardens were not maintained and restoration was necessary when, belatedly, the magnitude of their loss was recognized. This was accomplished in 1939-40 by the combined efforts of the Garden Club of Virginia and the Thomas Jefferson Memorial Foundation. In 1954-55, the Foundation restored additional beds with emphasis on bulb and tuber plantings. Wherever records made it possible the restorations are authentic and the remainder are conjectural restorations.

The long drive up the slopes to Monticello preserves the topography and natural growth of the area. Jefferson first deplored the lack of level surfaces which would accommodate gardens as they were then conceived. His genius worked out a plan for trimming lower limbs of the forest to create the effect of open areas which could then be enriched with underplantings.

The gardens themselves are deceptively simple in appearance unless they are viewed as part of the entity of design which is all of Monticello. The flower beds around the house, the round-about walk and border beds, the fishpool, the house, and the two pavilions all work together to form a unit of design whose parts, to be fully appreciated, must be taken in context. Everything reflects Jefferson's philosophy of unity between building architecture and landscaping. It is all in the character of an unpretentious genius whose words and deeds were in the service of a land and humanity he loved.

Jefferson provided an all-weather, covered passage from kitchen to house.

To many visitors Monticello's gardens are disappointingly simple until they see them in relation to the buildings.

Berkeley Plantation
Charles City County, Virginia

From their tiny ship moored at the edge of land granted by James I in 1618 to the Berkeley Company, the newly arrived settlers stepped ashore on December 4, 1619 and, in accordance with the Proprietors' instructions that "the day of our ship's arrival . . . shall be yearly and perpetually kept as a day of Thanksgiving," celebrated the first American Thanksgiving Day more than a year before the Pilgrims arrived in New England.

Berkeley continued to be a significant contributor to American history. One of its early owners, Col. Benjamin Harrison, was a member of the Continental Congress, signer of the Declaration of Independence, three times a Governor of Virginia, and close friend of George Washington. His son, William Henry Harrison, achieved fame as "Old Tippecanoe" and became the ninth President. His inaugural address was written at Berkeley. In William Henry's grandson, Benjamin Harrison, the house produced yet another President. It shares with the Adams House in Massachusetts the distinction of having housed two Presidents.

Along with its honors, Berkeley bears sorry marks of history. March 22, 1622 was the date of the first armed conflict between the settlers and the Indians in what later became the United States. It took place at Berkeley. The settlers were wiped out except for one child, Thomas Tracy, who later became Governor of Connecticut, having been taken to New England by his Indian captors.

In 1781, Berkeley was plundered by troops under the command of Benedict Arnold. During the Civil War it served as Headquarters for General McClellan after the Battle of Malvern Hill. While quartered here in the summer of 1862, General Butterfield composed "Taps." One hundred forty thousand Federal troops camped on these fields and gunboats anchored in the James River.

From the house to the river is a third of a mile of slope converted to a series of long terraces which housed pleasure gardens, kitchen gardens and orchards. The upper terraces were and are a large green garden of boxwood parterres. The lower levels were fruit and vegetable areas. Between these there was a transitional section which combined utilitarian and decorative uses.

The boxwood around the house and in the formal gardens is justly famed. Its ancestors were brought from England over 300 years ago. All the plants in the garden are 18th century and it is the intent to maintain this. Berkeley is deliberately not clipped and groomed because the owners want it to reflect the appearance it would have had in the years of the Harrisons' occupancy. Grass and shrubs were not clipped so close in the days of total dependence on manual labor and primitive instruments.

At the water's edge stands a façade replica of the ship Margaret which brought the settlers from Bristol, England. The setting is used as a background for an annual play reenacting the landing and Thanksgiving Celebration. The Berkeley Thanksgiving was an expression of thanks to the Lord for safe passage across the Atlantic. It is in contrast to the Plymouth Thanksgiving which was an expression of gratitude for having survived a difficult first year on the New England shore.

Berkeley and Westover are located near the first land road to the west, running from Williamsburg to Richmond.

Westover
Charles City County, Virginia

Like its close neighbor, Berkeley, Westover is reached by dirt road, which is intended to take visitors back in time as they approach the estates. One mile of this road to Westover is a double avenue of red cedar.

Westover was named for Henry West, fourth Lord Delaware and son of Thomas West, Governor of Virginia, but its importance to Virginia was greatened when, in 1688, it became the seat of the Byrd family.

Architecturally, the house is considered to be one of the outstanding examples of Georgian structures in America. Its simple elegance of form and proportion and its setting combine to make it the essence of Colonial Virginia style and quality. The entrance facing the river, copied numberless times, has given architects a decorative-functional feature still called "the Westover Doorway."

Just to the east of the house is the open brick-lined pit of the old icehouse, going down twenty-five feet. Just beyond is a small structure containing a dry well and a ladder to passageways leading to the basement of the house and to the river. These were escape tunnels to be used in case of Indian attack. The lower floor shutters of the house are constructed with slits through which guns could be fired on attackers.

Discreetly surrounded by tall boxwood is the brick "Necessary" with multiple seating arrangements that are a remarkable demonstration of togetherness. The presence of a fireplace is a most unusual concession to comfort in a Colonial "comfort station."

The famous Westover gates carry the initials WEB.
The eagles are a symbolic play on the name Byrd.

Three sets of wrought-iron gates to the north, the east, and the west of the house are especially noteworthy. Those to the north have the initials "WEB" incorporated into the design. The lead eagles that cap the gate columns are an emblematic play on the name "Byrd." The iron fence has fourteen columns each with its own stone finial of individual design and symbolic meaning.

The rectangular, wall-enclosed garden is divided into quarters by two walks; at the exact center where the paths cross is the large tomb of "the Black Swan of Westover," William Byrd II, builder of Westover and founder of Richmond,
buried in 1744.

The gardens are not so lovely as they once were. Nematodes have done considerable damage to the old boxwood and yaupon is being tried as a possible substitute for box hedging if a substitute should prove necessary. Where box was used as individual plantings it is being replaced with rhododendrons. It is to be hoped that these efforts will bring back the gardens whose beauty still struggles to shine through the blight.

Unusual to the low garden wall is the brick stile leading to the manager's cottage. The wall has three types of capping: one is semicircular, one is semi-octagonal, and one is semicircular with vertical sides.

From the house to the river slope is a broad stretch of lawn on which stands a spreading yew 54 feet in diameter. The east edge of the lawn is flanked by a curving walk banked with still healthy and beautiful boxwood. The slope to the river is covered with vetch whose tiny, magenta blossoms twinkle in the grass. Here is one of the tunnel exits, no longer serviceable after hundreds of years but no longer needed since there seems little chance that the Indian attack on adjacent Berkeley in 1622 will be repeated.

Above—Stile in the brick garden wall. Right —The Westover Doorway has become a standard for architects. It is an outstanding example of functional beauty.

Chippokes Plantation
Surry, Virginia

Chippokes is situated across the river from Jamestown, the first successful English settlement in the New World. It was named for a friendly Indian Chief. In the early records, his name was spelled in various ways but it is obvious that the plantation bears a version.

Through the more than 350-year existence of Chippokes the dominant feature has been its unbroken continuity as a producing farm of 1400 acres. Intact over the years, Chippokes' future has been insured by the generosity of its last private owner, Mrs. Evelyn Stewart, who gave the plantation, lands, buildings, and furnishings to the State of Virginia as a memorial to her husband. Both are buried in the gardens they built.

The gardens are six acres in size, surrounded by meadows, farm fields, and woods. There is not a feeling of formal symmetry here but an easy naturalness of growth which gives each plant full scope for development. Not to be seen elsewhere is the mass of crape myrtles in the gardens; where other gardens have used crape myrtle as an accent Chippokes has made them a principal feature. Chippokes differs from other James River plantation gardens in that they show closer ties to their British parenthood.

The front of the house faces the river almost a mile away. Flowering fruit trees and dogwoods have been placed to give an impression of random growth but each is in a position of maximum effectiveness to beautify the view of house or river.

The real gardens are behind the residence. As if to say, "See what I can do," a gigantic boxwood stands 20 feet tall with a diameter of 36 feet. All around are clumps and rows of the crape myrtle. Beneath the delicate pinks and sparkling whites of fruit trees and dogwoods, azaleas make a brilliant show above the delicacy of daffodils, narcissi, primroses, irises, forget-me-nots, mertensia, woods hyacinths, and star of Bethlehem.

The outbuildings and the working farm complete a picture of Virginia plantation life as it was in a rich past. The agricultural uses of the land, the lawns and gardens, the buildings, all are being maintained now by the Commonwealth as a State Park.

The front of Chippokes looks out on the meadows toward the James River.

Even as a state park Chippokes remains a working agricultural farm.

31

Brandon
Prince George County, Virginia

Up river from Chippokes is the large property called Brandon whose first Patent, which conveys 7,000 acres to John Martin, Esq., is dated 1616 and includes the names of Pembroke, Southampton, Francis Bacon, and John Smith.

Martin was a member of the original Council, having arrived in 1607. It is likely that Martin had begun farming Brandon well before the issuance of the Patent since, in that year, he sailed to England taking a full cargo of tobacco, potash, sturgeon, caviar and other commodities. It may well be that Brandon is the oldest continuous agricultural enterprise in the United States. It is, today, an operating farm.

Standing to the side of the residence hall is the brick "blockhouse" built as a defense against Indian attack. The main house was designed by Thomas Jefferson. It bears the bullet scars of the Revolutionary and the Civil Wars. They are all around the main door facing the river, 300 yards away, across the length of the gardens. The interior was not totally spared. A part of the living room panelling was burned as firewood before an officer put a stop to the vandalism.

Great, untrimmed box and English yews stand close to the house on all sides and give testimony to the garden's age. Across the lawn, framing the view of the river, are two huge cucumber trees and the remains of a row of pecan trees brought from the West Indies over 300 years ago. The remaining trunk of one of these felled by a hurricane is 23 feet in circumference. A gnarled mulberry is a reminder of the futile attempts to establish a silk industry in the Colonies.

Beyond the boxwood- and tulip poplar-lined lawn lies the garden of a series of box-edged parterres containing a full variety of seasonal blooms. These lead to the natural terrace above the broad expanse of the James.

The wife of the young owner of Brandon, Mrs. Robert W. Daniel, Jr., has taken on herself the awesome responsibility of

Impatiens and ivy brighten garden columns at Brandon.

maintaining the acres of a garden which has never needed restoration. She continues the traditional role of the Mistresses of Brandon in assuming primary responsibility for the gardens, leaving the men free to devote their time and efforts to the other, productive affairs of the plantation.

The gardens of Chippokes and Brandon have definite rectilinear patterns but the use of the plantings as natural, untrimmed growth is such as to create a feeling of order without the imposition of stern control. It is this which accounts for their great charm which could well be described as being truly "innocent." In societal structure it would be like a community of people with such regard for order that law and law enforcement would be unnecessary and redundant. This is the epitome of achievement—assurance without presumption or self-importance, beauty without artifice. It is nature and humanity in delightful harmony.

The south bank of the James River has never received the recognition given to the Jamestown side. Brandon and Chippokes, maintained intact and in prime beauty, make the south shore worthy of at least equal regard and attention.

Above
Brandon's Green Garden is a place apart.
Left
The main house at Brandon was designed by Thomas Jefferson.

Oatlands
Leesburg, Virginia

Northernmost of the gardens in this volume is Oatlands, an historic estate located a few miles below Leesburg in the hunt country of Virginia.

The hilliness of the Piedmont gives a special character to the gardens which are composed of a complex series of terraces which go down and around a sharp slope below the balustraded lawn of the Georgian mansion. There are seven levels in one direction and seven in another. Many of the levels contain individual parterres which gain in beauty and importance because, in addition to walk-through viewing, they can be seen from above and their overall designs more fully appreciated.

If any green garden in the world can be said to seriously challenge Gunston Hall it is Oatlands. Here is boxwood in the fullest variety of uses. Parterre hedges are impeccably groomed; tremendous growths form green canyons and tunnels; large individual plants take their natural forms and size; copses stand like small forests; some areas combine the box with yew in an effective mixing of texture and color.

The flower plantings in the several seasons are planned to perpetuate the riding colors of the late owner, William Corcoran Eustis. Spring hyacinths and daffodils or fall salvia and chrysanthemums flower in the colors of his mauve and yellow silks.

Oatlands reflects the work of two owners. The first, its builder, was George Carter, great grandson of King Carter who left an estate of 330,000 acres. George Carter's father bought 63,093 acres from the estate of Lord Fairfax. Five thousand of these acres he gave to George as a coming of age present in 1798. Two years later he began construction of the house and the development of seven acres of English boxwood gardens and bowling green.

George Carter lived at Oatlands as a bachelor until 1837. One morning of that year the widow Betty Lewis presented herself at the estate, her carriage having broken down near the gates. The courtly 60-year-old bachelor invited her to stay while repairs to the carriage were effected. He showed her the gardens' charms and was smitten by the widow's. He forthwith proposed marriage and she forthwith accepted. Two sons were born to this union which lasted till George's death nine years later.

The Civil War took its toll of Oatland's affluence and this, combined with the continued extravagance of Mrs. Carter and her younger son, spelled a period of hard times for the estate and the house and lands passed from the Carters to Stilson Hutchins, founder of the Washington *Post*. Hutchins

An old Italian wellhead is silhouetted against the sky.

never lived at Oatlands, which was boarded up, the gardens overgrown, and the fields untended.

In 1903, William Corcoran Eustis and his wife of three years rode out from their Washington home to see the estate. After three of these horse and buggy trips they decided to buy the property though they had not seen the inside of the house. They wanted it as a residence during the hunting season. Their Washington home was Corcoran House which Eustis had inherited from his grandfather, creator of the Corcoran Gallery of Art and founder of the Riggs National Bank.

For William Eustis, equestrian sportsman, Oatlands was a place for horsemanship, but, for Mrs. Eustis it was a place for gardening. She restored and extended George Carter's great gardens. Instead of rebuilding the bowling green which had degenerated into a potato patch she created the lovely boxwood allée.

Over the years until she died in 1964, Mrs. Eustis combined love of gardening with welfare work. Following her death Oatlands became the property of her daughters who, in 1965 gave the house, furnishings and 261 acres of surrounding land, with an endowment for preservation and maintenance to the National Trust.

Lawn bowling now takes place every Saturday during the long season on the terrace below the balustrade. Horse and pony shows, point-to-point racing and fox hunting are again a part of the Oatlands activities. Each April, the William Corcoran Eustis Cup goes to the winner of the timber race of the Loudon Hunt's Point-to-Point Meeting. Oatlands' own timber course was designed by Crompton "Tommy" Smith, grandson of a man against whom Eustis competed. Smith is the only American to win the English Grand National. The American Boxwood Society holds its annual meeting at Oatlands.

The interests and the joys of both the Eustises are preserved as is the Estate built by George Carter.

The one-time bowling green was rescued from its fate as a potato patch and became the boxwood allée.

Each of the terraces is distinguished by its own parterre design.

Agecroft
Windsor Farms, Richmond, Virginia

Well upriver from the plantation country on the James River, in a residential section of Richmond, stands an Elizabethan English house which was built before the voyage of Columbus to the New World. Called Agecroft Hall, it was built in the latter part of the 1400's by the descendants of the deLangley family which had come to England with William the Conqueror. Its architecture is a combination of early Gothic and early Renaissance in what was called "half-timbered construction." In its original form its walls were not so graced with windows as they were to be after it became more a manor house and less a fortress residence.

Agecroft was built near the site of the 12th century village "Achecroft," a name probably pronounced "aitchcroft" and then "agecroft."

Three years after Elizabeth I had become Queen of England, Agecroft was inherited by the daughter of Sir Robert deLangley and was thereafter passed on to her descendants, the Dauntseys. It was so solidly built that it withstood all of nature's assaults during the centuries it continued to stand in its native Lancashire. But, man succeeded where nature had failed. As nearby Manchester became increasingly industrialized, coal mines were opened all around the ancient house. Sinking pits filled with stagnant water while others made the building's foundations unstable. By 1925, Agecroft seemed doomed to fall before man-made decay or demolition. A Richmond man learned of this impending disaster and succeeded in buying the house. T. C. Williams, Jr., the buyer, announced his intent of moving Agecroft to Richmond, and a country which had been apathetic to the threat of loss by neglect and misuse became aroused to the threat of loss by exportation.

The hue and cry subsided when the venerable Manchester *Guardian* wrote that Agecroft Hall was "too reproachful a jewel to leave in that ruined landscape." The New York *Herald-Tribune* said, "A house that has crossed the ocean is presumably an object of some reverence. If we may picture Agecroft Hall queening it once more in ample meadows, with bright sunshine to throw up the clean gay pattern of its timbering . . . the rebirth will have its compensations."

It has been and still is revered. For forty years, Mrs. Daniel Morton, widow of the man who brought Agecroft to the James River shore, lived here and maintained it. The joy of knowing the house and insuring its continuing existence is sufficient compensation for Mrs. Morton who has

Walk from the formal garden to the garden house.

turned the property over to the Agecroft Association. Appropriate to Agecroft's heritage is the fact that the curator of the house is English and the gardener an English-born, naturalized American.

The striking facades of tall gables, white plaster and dark oak timbers, and rich mullioned windows are set off by cobblestone courts, English boxwood, broad lawns, and fine gardens.

Adjacent to the house on the river side is a great terrace whose magnificence is tempered by the modesty of the small terrace which overlooks the sunken garden seen through openings in the boxwood. The sunken garden was inspired by the Pond Gardens of the great Tudor estate, Hampton Court. Its character is different from most formal gardens. It is without parterre sections. As a result, it seems simpler in concept and more open than usual English-inspired formal gardens. But it is richly varied in texture and interest and color. To either side of the sunken garden are garden houses which repeat the architecture of the main house.

On the next level below the sunken garden is the formal garden, set apart by hedges, trees and walls covered with white wisteria. It consists of two levels of its own. The lower is the major section built around an armillary sphere standing above the bright floral displays of the beds. The upper terrace is blessed with the use of azaleas in the most delicate colors. A stairway leads up to a wrought-iron gateway to the long crape myrtle allée that parallels the length of the sunken garden on its river side. Above is the flagstone forecourt of the house whose walls and arches are framed by the purple of wisteria and green of boxwood.

Agecroft is a part of the England which sent its first colonists to America to Roanoke Island and to Jamestown. That the shore heights of the James River now provide haven to this Tudor building and Elizabethan garden speaks well for the historic ties between Virginia and England.

The entrance court at Agecroft.

Beyond the formal garden, down the lawned slopes,
is the James River.

NORTH CAROLINA

Orton Plantation
Near Wilmington, N.C.

Orton is located on the Cape Fear River on the opposite shore to the Cape itself about 16 miles below Wilmington. It is about a mile upriver from the site of old Brunswick Town.

There were several explorations of the Cape Fear area, so named because of the treacherous shoals and unsafe seas outside the mouth of the river. Exploration began in 1524 with Giovanni da Verrazano. Two years later Lucas Vasquez de Ayllon sailed from Hispaniola with six hundred settlers. One of the ships was lost at the mouth of the river and another was built to replace it. After a stay of only a few months the colony moved to Winyaw Bay on the South Carolina Coast. In 1561 the King of Spain decreed that no further attempts were to be made by Spain to colonize "Florida" as the territory was then known.

The Massachusetts Bay Colony explored Cape Fear in 1662 and 1663 but did not find it satisfactory. In the same years the British Colony at Barbados sent an exploration and in 1664 settled a colony twenty miles upriver from the sea. Difficulties caused its abandonment and by the end of 1667 the site was deserted.

Not until 1725 was further settlement attempted at Cape Fear's lower extremities. This was accomplished by another group of Barbadans joined by South Carolinians who wished to enjoy the low rates of taxation of North Carolina. A few years earlier the river mouth had been rid of the notorious pirate Captain Stede Bonnet who was defeated, captured, and taken to Charleston where he was hanged.

Brunswick Town was founded in 1725 by Maurice Moore on his grant on the west bank of the river. By 1727 a ferry was in operation. Things looked favorable for the area's development but Maurice soon sold the Orton land to his brother Roger who developed it into a great plantation and won himself the appelation "King" Roger because of his "masterful personality" and generosity. He became feared and respected by the Indians with whom he had many encounters. One tale has it that he, in the company of one of his men, captured a body of Indians after they had "frolicked drunkenly." Waiting till it was dark, Roger crossed the river and, finding the Indians asleep, caused the balls to be removed from their guns which were then put back as before. He then woke the Indians with shouts. They roused and took up their arms against the feared Moore and fired them at point blank range thinking to kill him then and there. To their consternation Moore stood unharmed and imperiously ordered them to throw down their weapons and surrender. Thinking Moore to bear a charmed life impervious to their arms they obeyed and were taken captive.

Because Orton was used as a hospital it was spared the destruction suffered by its neighbors in the Civil War.

Because of the great pine forests which provided what seemed to be a limitless supply of timber, spars, tar pitch and turpentine so necessary to wooden ships the area quickly prospered and Brunswick Town became an important port. In 1748 three Spanish ships fired on the town. The Spaniards landed and looted the town. The colonists counterattacked, sank one ship, took captives, and forced the Spaniards to leave their booty and withdraw.

In 1776, the British looted and burned the town and several plantations. Brunswick Town was destroyed and was never rebuilt. Orton was spared though its neighbors were razed.

During the Civil War the Federal troops used Orton House as a hospital for their sick and wounded and again the antebellum mansion was spared the destruction suffered by its neighboring plantations. Like "King" Roger Moore, its founder, Orton seems to have led a charmed life brought to its present state of beauty by the late James Sprunt who bought it from his father-in-law for his wife Luola Murchison Sprunt.

Among Dr. Sprunt's philanthropies was the establishment of a Missionary school in China. His interest in the Orient is reflected in at least one area of the Gardens, an angulated bridge which bears a sign

> "The Ancient Chinese . . . believed that evil spirits followed them but could not turn. The crooked bridges forced the evil spirits to fall overboard and drown."

Dr. Sprunt encouraged his wife to add the wings to Orton House and to begin designing and planting the gardens. The lovely little chapel which greets visitors is a memorial to Luola Sprunt.

With the exception of the sunken scroll garden, the entire area is quite informal and natural in its appearance. Even the scroll garden is not so elaborate or ornate as these usually are. Its form follows the natural contours of its setting whose irregularities are brought into complete harmony by the complementary shapes of the planting beds and scroll-formed hedges.

James Laurence Sprunt, son of the man and woman who created the expanded gardens, tells how the scroll design of the lower garden came into being: Robert Swann Sturtevant, a New Englander, had drawn several plans for this section after it had been washed out by hurricane waters. Neither he nor the Sprunts were satisfied with his efforts. One day, Sturtevant was resting on a sofa in the living room and Mrs. Sprunt covered him with a paisley coverlet. He looked at its design for a little while and jumped up with a shout. "That's it," he cried. The shapes of the paisley design became the scroll outlines of green which house the color of the bedding plants and a cycle was complete. A cycle which began with Kashmiri artists applying nature-inspired designs to cloth; continued with the adoption of the design by Scottish weavers; and came full circle at Orton with the design being given back to the nature which first inspired it.

"King" Roger's tomb is at one end of the garden in an old, Colonial burying ground. His charmed life ended but the charm of the gardens and the house he built go on. At the reception center or at the house there is real warmth in the hospitality extended to the visitor, whether he be human or bird. The old plantation rice fields are now a wildfowl refuge and Orton's foliage is rich with the color and the song of winged visitors.

With its tidewater location, its climate, and its varied features Orton Plantation combines in one place the things for which its more famous neighbors to the south are individually noted.

A winter which has been difficult for camellias brings no complaint here. Mr. Sprunt says, "Yes, it has been a rough year for camellias and some of the early bloomers, but what a blessing it has been for lawns. I don't know when they have looked so lush and green." It is that kind of place—where everything seems to be for the best.

Bridge crosses the river inlet to the marsh flats.

Tryon Palace
New Bern, N.C.

"Have your mind at peace
With a heart that will not harden
From worry and sorrow find release
In a Tryon Palace garden."

Royal Governor William Tryon had as his first residence in North Carolina, Russellborough at Brunswick Town, just to the south of Orton Plantation. In February of 1766, his house was surrounded by five hundred Cape Fear men who forced the resignation and withdrawal of the Stamp Master, Mr. Pennington. This was one of the first overt acts of rebellion against the hated Stamp Act, which also precipitated the Boston Tea Party.

To locate his residence closer to the center of activity Governor Tryon moved his government to New Bern, located at the confluence of the Neuse and Trent Rivers. Here, he had built in 1767-70 the Georgian "Palace" which was described by contemporaries as "the most beautiful building in the Colonial Americas." The main building was destroyed by fire in 1798, four years after the State Capital had been moved from New Bern to Raleigh. A street was cut through the Palace Square and lots on both sides were sold by the State. More than 40 structures were built on those lots. The east wing of the Palace disappeared but the west wing (stable building) survived.

Restoration of the Palace on its original foundations was accomplished in 1952-59, principally with gifts and bequests of the late Mrs. James Edwin Latham of Greensboro, a native New Bernian.

Fortunately, the drawings and specifications of the original architect, "Master Builder" John Hawks, were found in New York and England and made possible the authentic restoration of the buildings. A detailed inventory of Gov. Tryon's furnishings was also available and greatly assisted in the furnishing of the interior.

Since no such records or description of the gardens were obtainable the Tryon Palace Commission decided to create gardens like those which flourished in 1760 to 1770 in Great Britain. Drawings of numerous gardens executed in that period are extant and made it possible for Morley Williams to design a lovely setting for the Palace which is authentic to the time of its building and occupancy. Mr. Williams enclosed the gardens within high walls as was done in the 18th Century. The walls tempered cool winds and reflected sunshine as well as insuring privacy. Privy gardens within the compound were themselves enclosed and were meant to be enjoyed from the windows of the house and were accessible only to its occupants. The walls served as backgrounds and supports for the espaliered dwarf fruit trees and grape vines which were popular in those days. Tryon Palace has two privy gardens.

Ornamental and kitchen gardens, while notably different in purpose and design, did not exclude the mingling of plantings— flowers and flowering plants were grown along with vegetables and herbs in the kitchen gardens while herbs and simples were grown in the most decorative flower gardens. This practice has been followed in the Palace Gardens.

The most elaborate of the gardens is the Maude Moore Latham Garden on the west side of the grounds. There is a white memorial pavilion with a plaque marking her achievement in bringing about the rebirth of Tryon Palace and its grounds. This is a superb ornamental garden of English design with colorful flower beds in various shapes bordered by clipped dwarf yaupon, surrounded by intricate brick walks. Four Italian marble statues representing the four seasons are the dominant stone pieces.

On the east side of the main building is the larger of the privy gardens, the Kellenberger Garden (Mrs. Kellenberger is the only daughter of Mrs. Latham). It is much simpler in design than the Latham Garden. By the walls are redwood trellises on which yellow jessamine, confederate jessamine, cruel vines, and pyracantha form a backdrop for the colorful flower beds whose plantings are changed with the seasons.

The other privy garden is on the west side of the house. The Green Garden is formal with low, shaped hedges of dwarf yaupon between gravel walks, cornered by four clipped cherry laurels. Crape myrtles grow at the western end. There are beds of periwinkle bordered by santolina. In the center of the evergreens is a limestone statue, "Boy with Grapes," formerly in Mrs. Latham's private garden.

Honoring the architect of the original buildings is Hawks Allée, named for John Hawks. On the brick wall at the front are white cherokee roses. The lawn is bordered by low, flowering plants such as lilies and lilies of the valley and by tall, clipped holly trees. The five antique Italian statues of Roman gods and goddesses came from the garden of the sister-in-law of a direct descendant of John Hawks. Adjacent to Hawks Allée is the Pleached Allée of yaupon trained over a tall arch to make a lovely arbor whose southern end provides a fine vista of the Trent River.

The south grounds are a great expanse of lawn flanked by the East and West Wilderness areas. One of the two flagpoles near the water flies the British Red Ensign which was used by England when North Carolina was a colony. The other pole flies a replica of the Stars and Stripes carried by the Tar Heel Militiamen at the Battle of Guilford Courthouse in 1781. It is said that this was the only Stars and Stripes actually borne by American troops during the Revolutionary War.

The kitchen garden to the east of the kitchen wing is substantial in size and planting, noteworthy for its large collection of espaliered pear, apple, quince and fig trees. Indian corn is grown from seed provided by Tuscarora Indians who were driven away from their Carolina homes to New York in Colonial days.

The loggia arches to both sides of the front of the Palace.

Entry to the Kellenberger Garden from the loggia.

Bright-leaf tobacco is grown, dried and hung in the nearby smokehouse with other dried plants, herbs, and smoked meats.

The Work Garden, near the Green Garden, is adjacent to the poultry house, dovecote, well and garden shop. Here is one of the two 18th Century English piston-type pumps which draw water without priming.

On their original sites, two reconstructed pentagonal "Necessary Houses," one on each side of the Palace, are approached by brick walks lined with hawthorn hedges, and plantings of ivy, oxalis, and other flowering plants.

Almost all of the plants in the north areas of the Palace grounds are of purely American ancestry.

Across the street from the Palace are the auditorium with its own gardens and four other houses restored as part of the Palace Restoration complex. Each of these has its own notable gardens.

Tryon Palace, its gardens, and its environs are a magnificent recapturing of the past for which Mrs. Kellenberger received, among many honors, the coveted Crowninshield Award of the National Trust for Historic Preservation for "superlative achievement in the preservation and interpretation of sites and buildings significant in American history and culture." That it also is grandly beautiful is as important as its authenticity and history.

The knot garden is a marvel of precise design and maintenance of form.

Maude Moore Latham Gardens at Tryon are perhaps the largest and most elaborate of the Baroque expression in gardening to be seen anywhere.

Elizabethan Garden, Manteo
Roanoke Island, N.C.

Created and maintained by The Garden Club of North Carolina, Inc., The Elizabethan Garden is located on the north end of Roanoke Island near Manteo, adjacent to historic Fort Raleigh and the spot where the "Lost Colony" was established in 1587. This garden is a memorial to the Elizabethan colonists who attempted the first English settlement in America.

Built on ten and a half acres of indigenous growth, the Garden is a concept of the kind of pleasure garden the homesick Elizabethan colonists might have created had the settlement endured.

The dedication ceremony which formally opened the Garden took place on August 18, 1960, the 373rd anniversary of the birth of Virginia Dare, granddaughter of Governor John White, and the first child of English parentage born in America.

The colonists were left to their own (inadequate) devices for a period of almost three years because Elizabeth I and England were engaged in war with Spain and the defeat of the Spanish Armada. The ships which came in 1590 to relieve the colonists found the houses dismantled and the settlement area enclosed within a high palisade. On a prominent post near the palisade entrance the bark had been peeled off and the letters CROATOAN carved into the wood. The prearranged distress or forced departure sign, a cross, was absent. It was assumed that the colonists would be found on Croatoan Island or among the friendly Croatoan Indians inland. No search was possible at the time and subsequently there was found no trace of the missing colonists other than the Indian legends which spoke of "the white doe," thought to be the child, Virginia Dare.

A few years ago two North Carolina ladies were showing a British visitor the Lost Colony area when he remarked that it would be an ideal place for a memorial garden. From this seed the idea took root and grew into a beautiful garden unique in its combination of Elizabethan form and indigenous flora and fauna.

Visitors first see the Raleigh gatehouse modeled after the architecture of Hayes Barton, home of Raleigh in England. Inside is authentic English furniture of the period and a 1590 oil portrait of Elizabeth I attributed to Zuccaro; a rare book of reproductions of Royal Governor John White's water color drawings of flora and fauna of the area (he was the first resident naturalist); the National awards won by the Garden; and parchment copies of the lists of the members of the first and second colonies.

On the brick walls (fashioned of bricks made by Silas Lucas, generally credited with being the first brickmaker in America) is a large plaque stating the inspiration and intent of the Garden and its creators.

> The Elizabethan Garden—Down the Centuries English Women have built gardens to the Glory of God, the beauty of the Countryside and the comfort of their souls. The Women of The Garden Club of North Carolina, Inc. have planted this Garden in memory of the valiant men and women who founded the first English Colony in America. From this hallowed ground on Roanoke Island, they walked away through the dark forest, and into History. 1585-1953.

The imposing wrought-iron gates once stood at the French Embassy in Washington. Inside, one is greeted by the fragrance of the herb garden where 32 herbs, medicinal and culinary, are grown. Rosemary, Queen Elizabeth's favorite which she carried to sniff, is abundant here. There is a fine old Italian stone fountain which is used by many as a wishing well.

Flower- and shrub-bordered walks lead to the Uppowoc (tobacco) beds and then to the Octagonal Mount, a natural small hill which was a characteristic eminence employed in old English gardens. At the center of the Mount is an ancient pink marble sculptured well-head. From the Mount various aspects of the Garden may be viewed in all directions. To the north, Roanoke Sound may be seen.

Across the water, the dunes of the outer banks and Kitty Hawk are clearly visible. To the east, in bold relief against the dark background of windswept pines, hollies and oaks, stands the statue of Virginia Dare as an adult waif of the woods and sea. The otherwise nude figure is draped with fishnet and wears arm and neck laces of Indian beads.

Carved in Rome by Louise Landers in 1859, the sculpture was lost in a Mediterranean shipwreck. It was, after two years, salvaged by the Italian government and reclaimed (for a price) by Louise Landers who kept it at her homes in Boston and Washington. She willed it to the State of North Carolina which had expressed an interest in this example of its history. The state subsequently gave it to Pulitzer-prize winner Paul Green in appreciation of his writings on North Carolina. He, in turn, gave the statue to the Elizabethan Garden which displays it on the spot where Virginia Dare once played as a child.

To the south are the open, games lawns. To the west is the sunken knot garden, a copy of a Shakespeare garden which is the formal highlight of the entire garden. Quadrated, each of the eight bed sections is centered by one of four statues representing Apollo, Diana, Venus and Zeus. The parterre shapes are outlined with clipped Heller's holly and are filled according to season with pansies for winter and spring, petunias, ageratum, and begonias for summer and fall—all accented by crape myrtle.

The overall square is enclosed by a low, perforated brick wall which is itself enclosed by a pleached allée of clipped yaupon shaped to form viewing "windows."

The center of the knot garden is a magnificent ancient Italian fountain whose

circular balustrade bears the Farnese coat of arms. The fountain pedestal is capped by a female figure. This fountain is thought to be the work of Michelangelo who is known to have executed such works for the Farnese Palace near Rome. This and many other fine sculptures were the gifts of former Ambassador to the Court of Saint James, John Hay Whitney.

The water gate leads to the shore of Roanoke Sound whose breezes keep the climate of the island temperate.

The fountain which centers the Elizabethan Garden is attributed to Michelangelo.

To the north of the sunken garden is the overlook terrace which provides a great view of the sound. To either side and below are intimate walkways through plantings of wild flowers and wind gnarled live oaks.

At the water's edge is evidence of the superintendent's love of and attention to nature. Louis Midgett had noticed that the sea was eroding the shoreline and cutting into the garden area. Mr. Midgett has succeeded not only in stopping the incursion but through employing nature's own forces has reversed the action to reclaim 60 feet of shore depth. Midgett had noted that where live oaks had fallen because of erosion the sea piled sand over them and rebuilt the shore. He obtained discarded old utility poles and built a series of breakwaters which he calls "groins." They are now completely covered by sea-deposited sand.

This work is typical of the accomplishment of a garden which has worked with nature to stabilize and enhance the natural beauty of a lovely place. The almost-extinct sea holly is being carefully nurtured here and is responding to love in a hospitable setting. Some of the live oaks were here when the colonists first took this ground. They should be here for many years to come.

The Elizabethan Garden is the result of love and generosity with a minimum expenditure of money; it is one of the good results of people coming together in concerted effort to note and preserve history, beauty, and most importantly, nature.

Aside from its uniqueness of Elizabethan design in America the Garden offers something far beyond its great visual beauty which includes hundreds of kinds of butterflies and birds. It offers beauty of sound in a natural symphony of wind soughing through trees, boom and hiss of surf on sand, and song of birds in a happy place.

From the wellhead on the Mount the view to the west looks down the walks to the sunken, knot garden.

Rhododendron and partridge berry share an unusual bedding place in the crotch of an old live oak.

Biltmore House and Gardens
Asheville, N.C.

Abutting Asheville is the Town of Biltmore Forest whose land was once a part of the huge Biltmore Estate. This is the Blue Ridge Mountain Country where, in 1888, George Washington Vanderbilt began the purchase of 125,000 acres of farms, woods and forested mountainsides. Of that acreage some 11,000 acres remain as part of the Estate. A large portion was deeded, after Mr. Vanderbilt's death in 1914, to the U.S. Government as the nucleus of Pisgah National Forest. Part of the remainder was developed into the Village and part sold for the Blue Ridge Parkway. Rights of way were granted to Interstate Routes 26 and 40. Conditions in selling and granting rights of way were that all sections of the roads which traverse Biltmore Estate be landscaped and maintained free of billboard or other advertising display and that bridge overpasses be designed in keeping with the gardens and be faced with stone.

The lodge gate provides entry to the Estate over three miles of winding approach road that runs through splendid plantings of pine, hemlock, hardwoods, rhododendron and mountain laurel in natural groupings. Over stone bridges, under highway bridge overpasses, past pools, around a final sharp turn to the wrought-iron gates and the great Esplanade. Facing the esplanade lawn is the massive Rampe Douce, a Renaissance concept of easy rise up a steep embankment. Above the Rampe is a long, steep rise of grassy slope up to a pergola housing a statue of Diana the Huntress who poses no threat to the deer which freely graze the slope. From the pergola is a breathtaking Olympian view of the house and the blue mountains beyond.

The Esplanade avenues, lined with tulip trees, lead to and from the imposing house of 250 rooms. The main entrance is flanked by small courts. Inside is the sunken Palm Court, filled in all seasons with flowers, palms and ferns.

A visitor to the Estate asked his guide whether Biltmore was an attempt to create a private Central Park (New York). The reply brought forth the information that Frederick Law Olmsted, who designed Central Park, also created the original plan for Biltmore. Five years and thousands of men were required for the basic construction and planting. On Olmsted's death in 1903, his work was taken over by Chauncey Delos Beadle, who served as Superintendent of Biltmore Estate for sixty years.

At one end of the house is the library terrace covered with wisteria and trumpet creeper borne on a fine wrought-iron trellis. The terrace looks out on what was the bowling green that now holds the immense swimming pool surrounded by fine lawn and boxwood hedge. At one corner is a gazebo from which can be viewed the steep drop to the valley across which is Mt. Pisgah National Forest.

Iron gates frame the Rampe Douce, a monumental stairway.

To the left, down a few steps, lies the long Italian Garden with three formal pools. The first contains the sacred lotus of Egypt, the second, unusual aquatic plants, and the third, water lilies. To the left the stonework wall is covered with ivy brought from Kenilworth Castle. Along the right side of the Italian Garden is an unusual mixed hedge of American holly and hemlock.

A broad, stone stairway leads down to the large pergola whose lateral members are of huge lead-capped beams. It is completely covered by wisteria which grows out from the wall at cross beam height. The tinkling fountains and deep shade of the pergola make this a cool retreat on the hottest summer days. Below and beyond lies the extensive Shrub Garden whose winding paths go past the flowering growth to the gateway of the four-acre Walled Garden.

Espaliered trees and shrubs grow flat against the wall. Weeping cherry, double dogwood and crab apple contribute to the color.

February brings the first color to the perennial borders, followed by daffodils, tulips, peonies, iris and a variety of other choice flowering plants. The season is brought to a late close with the brilliance of massed chrysanthemums. Summer bedding plants, grown in the "pattern" beds, do their blooming during the months when the perennials are out of flower.

The lower half of the Walled Garden contains the Rose Garden where about 7000 roses are grown. A Test Garden displays trial growths of new varieties.

On three walls there is an unusual planting combination. English ivy grows on the wall and a few inches away are climbing roses which make a lattice of bloom against the ivy.

The Conservatory and Greenhouses provide plants for the Palm Court, cut flowers for display in the mansion, and plants for bedding in the Walled Garden.

Drives and walking trails go down the wooded slope to the Azalea Garden which is a monument to Chauncey Beadle. He considered native azaleas to be the finest American shrubs and gathered, for over ten years, the largest and only complete collection in existence. In 1940, he gave the collection to Biltmore Estate where it was moved and dedicated to him. In addition to the natives, there are many Asiatic and hybrid azaleas, metasequoias, magnolias and the magnificent evergreens which remain in what was once a pinetum.

Farther down, at the right, is the Bass Pond with a bridge walk over the spillway at the far end. The spillway itself is a dramatic fall of water to the rocks of the gully below. At the stream level is one of the largest cypress trees in cultivation at this latitude and elevation. Downstream from the tree, its knees rise from the water in an extended row—like sentry pickets.

The forests on the present Estate and on Mt. Pisgah are an important part of American nature conservation history. The land east of the French Broad River was badly eroded, worn out farm soil. The few trees were largely weedy volunteers or badly defective. Many of these had to be removed to make space for planting of desirable types which form the present woodlands, so well established that it is difficult to believe that they were set around the turn of the century. This work was under the direction of America's first trained forester, Gifford Pinchot. The result was the first comprehensive forest plan devised in the Western Hemisphere. The magnitude of the continuing project called for full-time supervision and Dr. C.A. Schenck was brought from his post at the University of Darmstadt in Germany to be Chief Forester. He founded the Biltmore School of Forestry which, until it was discontinued at the start of World War I, trained many of the foresters who dominated the field in this country for many years. In the Mt. Pisgah Section Dr. Schenck developed the basis for "land use" concept of forestry and conservation in America. Some of the early experimental plots continue to be subjects for study by the U.S. Forestry Service.

Elizabethean Gardens, North Carolina

Biltmore, North Carolina

Mount Vernon, Virginia

Monticello, Virginia

Brandon, Virginia

Biltmore, North Carolina

The drives continue for several miles through the Biltmore Dairy Farms whose 1500 purebred Jersey cattle make up one of the largest and finest dairy herds in the world.

The production of this large herd brought about the development of Biltmore Dairy Farms, one of the largest dairies in the South. A new processing and manufacturing plant in Biltmore Village provides employment and a sound economic base for the town and an outlet for over 300 dairy farms of the area. Mr. Vanderbilt believed that lands should be productive as well as beautiful and the Dairy Farms give the Estate a utilitarian purpose in addition to the esthetic value of the House and its gardens.

Whatever Mr. Vanderbilt's motivations for creating what he hoped would be the finest country home in America, the end result was a National Forest, a foundation stone for conservation, a magnificent mansion filled with great treasures, and a lovely garden.

The monumental Rampe Douce is a series of six inclines which serve as stairway and retaining wall.

Old Salem Restoration
Winston-Salem, N.C.

Salem, the name of the Moravian Settlement now restored in Winston-Salem, was taken from the Hebrew word Shalom, meaning "peace." The threat, in 1947, that a supermarket was planned to be built in the heart of historic Old Salem, aroused Winston-Salem to the desirability of restoring and preserving the atmosphere and appearance of the settlement around which the city grew.

The Moravians were one of the first of the Protestant groups whose faith was founded on the preachings of Jan Hus, the Bohemian martyr who was burned at the stake in the 15th century. This was a persecuted faith which, in the early 1700s found refuge in Saxony where the Unity of Brethren, as they were called, gained new strength and established many of the traditions which exist today. The first Moravian settlement in the New World was in Georgia, but it was soon abandoned for colonies in Pennsylvania, where Bethlehem was the principal one.

In the early 1750s, the last of the Lords Proprietors of North Carolina, Lord Granville, happily sold the Brethren a tract of almost 100,000 acres which they named Wachovia. The first settlers came from Pennsylvania in 1753 and began to build a temporary town they called Bethabara (house of passage). After Bethabara was well established the Central, or Congregation Town, Salem was begun in 1766. It was to be a planned community in many respects: gravity-flow running water, the squares, building lots, the graveyard called "God's Acre."

Being a congregation town the residents' economic as well as spiritual affairs were directed by the Church. The congregation was divided into "choirs" according to sex, age and marital status. There were choirs of single brothers, single sisters, married people, widowers, widows, older boys, older girls, little boys and little girls. Even in burial a simplified choir system was observed: all men in one section, women in another, little boys in another, little girls in yet another.

The Gemein Rath, or Congregational Council, decided the important affairs of the Community. Every citizen, man or woman was a voter.

Business affairs were conducted by the Diaconie whose revenues came from lot and land rentals, interest on money and tools lent, church dues and fees, and from the community controlled businesses. These consisted, in Salem's early days, of the Tavern, the Red Tannery, the Community Store, the Mill and the Pottery.

Individual choirs had their own diaconies. The single brothers ran the brewery, the distillery, the slaughterhouse and an extensive farm.

Salem was assigned 4000 acres of the 100,000 acre Wachovia tract. This land was not sold to the inhabitants but was leased at a low rate in a leasehold system.

Behind the manufactory Miksch maintained his herb garden now restored.

Commercial or business activities were assigned to Brethren. Thus, the Winklers were the bakers and Johann Matthew Miksch became the tobacconist. Miksch was also permitted to engage in the sale of seed, spices and herbs. His wife was the only one in Salem permitted to sell gingerbread. Miksch had been a gardener in Holland and it was reflective of the practicality of the Brethren that he should be involved in the sale of things he knew most about and involvement that required a garden. This he established behind the manufactory where he cured and prepared tobacco for sale.

Johann Miksch's garden has been restored as he knew it in the 1770s. House and garden reflect the Moravians' deft use of their love of beauty and decoration in practical ways.

There is no record or evidence that there was a medicinal garden in Old Salem though there was, at Bethabara, a ninety-foot-square planting of ninety-six varieties of medicinal plants and herbs. It is thought that the Salem doctors supplied their own professional needs from their individual gardens.

The restored tavern dispenses excellent food of the Moravian cuisine, fine service and authentic atmosphere with waiters and waitresses garbed in pre-Revolutionary War attire. Current hairstyles eliminate the need for long-haired wigs for the young men. Out of keeping with strict adherence to Moravian customs, but a welcome innovation at the Tavern, is the new terrace for outdoor eating under a large wisteria arbor in the pleasant garden.

Another apparent paradox in Old Salem is the Contemporary Art Gallery housed in the old bank building. Its presence is actually appropriate since the artists exhibited here reflect an adventurous development not unrelated to that of the Brotherhood when they established their religious order. This, along with the Moravian's love of the decorative arts, gives the gallery good justification for its location, albeit in sharp contrast with the rest of Old Salem.

The restoration of Old Salem has been accomplished in such a way as to truly maintain the atmosphere of the days when it was established. It is a cherished piece of history which can be seen and felt to remind Americans that America was a land which gave welcome haven and promise to those multitudes who were not always welcome in their original homelands because they were "different."

Between the Community Store and The Old Salem Store there is a small piece of land which has been planted as a tiny, formal garden. Fittingly, it is very simple in design and functions as a small oasis of green between brick walls and walks. It is a demonstration of what could be done with small pieces of open ground in cities more in need than Salem of the "green islands of nature" which could be grown among the rock and cement and asphalt deserts.

The Miksch Tobacco Shop where herbs and seeds were sold. It is the oldest home in the Old Salem restoration.

Elevated view shows the extreme economy of design which is fitting to so small a garden.

Reynolda Gardens
Winston-Salem, North Carolina

Fifty-four years ago the Reynolds family moved into the bungalow on what was to become the Reynolds Estate.

Mrs. Katherine Reynolds was an idealist who planned a demonstration farm that would show the people of the area that there were better ways of making an agricultural living than following a mule through a tobacco patch. Her husband began to buy up small farms to provide land for her purpose.

Mr. and Mrs. Reynolds had met when she, a Mt. Airy girl, won first prize of $1,000 for her letter in a competition praising the Reynolds Tobacco Company products. A year later they were married. The records do not show whether Katherine's letter was based on firsthand familiarity with Reynolds' products.

By 1911, most of the land, 1200 acres at its largest, had been acquired for the estate.

In addition to the farm Mrs. Reynolds wanted a garden. It was first laid out by a New York man but Mrs. Reynolds was not satisfied with his efforts and, in 1917, she engaged Thomas W. Sears of Philadelphia who redesigned the gardens into three parts: the cut-flower garden, the formal, English-type flower garden, and the greenhouses.

The model farm project continued concurrently with the development of the gardens and accounts for the variety of specialized buildings on the estate. There were the Irish potato house, the sweet potato house, the poultry house, swine shelters, sheepcotes (the sheep grazed Mr. Reynolds' private nine-hole golf course), the blacksmith's shop, and three large barns.

During the summer months while the house was being built, the Reynolds family camped in tents in front of the construction as she personally supervised the work. They moved into the manor house late in 1917.

The self-sufficient estate provided all the food for the family and the staff. A cannery was operated and its surplus was shipped to military camps all through America's participation in World War I. The agricultural farm, however, was found to be economically costly and it was abandoned as Mrs. Reynolds turned her energies toward education and established a private elementary school on the estate.

The school was only one of Reynolda's cultural activities. Famous artists were brought here to perform and exhibit their work. This educational-cultural tradition has carried on over the years and has resulted in the creation of the Smith Reynolds and the Mary Reynolds Babcock Foundations. It was here that Wake Forest College was persuaded to move.

Mr. Babcock, husband of the late Mary Reynolds, dismembered the estate as carefully and with the same concern for purpose as had gone into its assemblage. The key consideration and guide has been that Reynolda and Reynolda House should continue their constructive, community roles. Four hundred acres were given to the Wake Forest Campus;

The texture of Cryptomeria trunks is as interesting as the foliage.

71

100 acres are maintained as the gardens; 13.5 acres are Reynolda Village; 160 acres are the Old Town Golf Course; the part of the estate that was Graylyn was given to the Bowman Gray School of Medicine, a part of Wake Forest University. Most of these philanthropic gifts were conceived to be income productive but, in the case of the gardens which are not, a fund was created to finance the Babcock Chair of Botany whose holder, Dr. Walter Flory, is responsible for the garden's maintenance.

In 1964, Reynolda House, Inc. was created as a non-profit organization established to: "Preserve, operate and maintain Reynolda House as a center for the encouragement of the arts and higher education; Provide headquarters and facilities for the Piedmont University Center; Encourage and advance the arts; Cultivate and encourage enlightenment in the history of this region and this state."

In 1911, Jess Anthony went to work at Reynolda. In 1959 he retired but two years later was asked to return as chief gardener, a post he filled until his death when he was in his eighties, after 58 years of service to the gardens. The long devotion of such black men as Jess Anthony accounts for the continued existence of many of the large gardens of the American south. As their ranks thin, it becomes increasingly difficult to maintain these beds of beauty.

Of the original gardens there are, today, two sections. The cut-flower gardens are largely used for experimental growths.

The great, rectangular formal garden remains the primary feature at Reynolda. A border of delicate cherry blossoms vies with the rows of magnolias whose large blooms point skyward as in defiance of late frosts while daffodils and tulips brighten the surface areas below pergolas and arbors. Two rows of large cryptomeria frame the long view from greenhouse entry to the reflecting pool. Along the walk by the conservatory peonies and anemones fill the beds with bright color. The green of

the garden is imposing but much of the original design has been lost as size of the mature shrubs has gained dominance. This is not necessarily bad but the character of a formal English garden which was the original intent has been greatly diminished, if not lost. In its own way the present state of the garden offers an American individuality rooted in its English ancestry.

The wisteria pergola is at the house end of the garden.

Large boxwood forms a base for magnolias in bloom.

Sarah P. Duke Gardens
Durham, N.C.

A bowl-like depression on the campus of Duke University was the site selected in 1932 by the late Dr. Frederic M. Hanes for a great garden to be enjoyed by students and visitors.

Dr. Hanes owned an exceptional collection of irises which became the garden's first planting. John C. Wister of Philadelphia drew the original plans whose realization was made possible by Sarah Duke's generosity.

Mrs. Duke's daughter, Mary Duke Biddle, contributed to the development and completion of an enlarged plan as a memorial to her mother. Mrs. Ellen Shipman of New York designed the terraced gardens and engaged the services of Frederic Leubuscher, an outstanding rock garden specialist, to create the rock garden in an area selected by Mrs. Shipman.

The juxtaposition of the formal terraces and the rock garden across the water lily pool provides a key to the various aspects of the overall philosophy that combines formality, transitional areas of less formal design and natural growth to effectuate the Gardens' three objectives: to provide a collection of plants for the enjoyment of the university community and the general public; to serve as a practical demonstration of the kinds of plants that will flourish here; to serve as a trial ground for new plants and new cultivation methods suitable to the area.

In all of the development, Dr. Hanes' guiding hand and inspiration continued to play an important part. His collection of irises is now replanted in the Hanes Memorial Iris Garden, incorporated in the master plan prepared in 1958 by W.B.S. Leong, landscape architect of Boston and Andover, Massachusetts. Mr. Leong is the planning consultant who assists in the implementation of the grand design. The work is enabled to proceed because of the foundation created by Mrs. Biddle to insure the future of the garden.

There is relatively little garden sculpture at Duke Gardens but what there is is excellent. Notable are the garden gates fabricated by Joseph Barnes. They are abstract, metallic sculptures used like stained glass. The flat metal panels brazed to the skeletal structure were chemically treated to create a variety of color patinas whose reflected tones heighten the relationship to stained glass. On these panels are abstract or non-objective, non-representational forms as well as a number of ancient universal symbols expressive of man, earth, friendship of men, family and various parts of nature.

A long walk leads to the circular rose garden and then to the great terraced garden which is entered through a wisteria pergola overlooking the terraces, pool and rock

View of terraced gardens across water lily pool.

garden. There is a lesson to be learned from the pergola which needs repainting—a repainting made almost impossible because of the thickness of the wisteria growth. For anyone planning a wisteria pergola it would be well to use a material which will not need paint or other impermanent finish.

In the terraces, the stone retaining walls and the planting are composed as a kind of visual counterpoint where the texture, color and form of one is used to emphasize the best features of the other.

There has been no great effort to introduce rare or exotic growth but Richard Fillmore, the horticulturist associate director, grew from seed imported from China just before Communist ascension to power, the Dawn Redwoods which are so unusual. They are deciduous conifers with foliage similar to that of the Bald Cypress. Like the cypress, the Dawn Redwood's trunk base has a notable bulge. In the Redwood, the bulge has a unique sculptural look because of the irregularity of forms which overlay each other.

Care is taken to extend the blooming period of the garden to the maximum, though Duke's elevation and latitude make it more difficult than elsewhere. Plants which, in the winter months, carry bright berries are used to contrast with evergreen foliage, and deciduous trees are given the fullest opportunity to display their leafless grace and structure.

These fifty acres of natural bowl have given much joy to many, and their usefulness is being extended by the development of additional nature areas such as the Fern Garden and the Azalea Court behind the wisteria pergola. The Sky Garden, a broad expanse of open lawn, is a forest glade to the south of the lily pool. It gives a sunlit lawn area used by many students for peaceful, outdoor studying and for some classes held alfresco. It is all an ideal idyll which serves to remind man that his knowledge and efforts must be kept in harmony with the universe of nature of which he is only a humble part.

The rock garden is on the slope opposite the main gardens.

Dawn redwood grow at Duke from seed obtained from China just before Communist accession to power.

SOUTH CAROLINA

Middleton Place
Charleston Area

Middleton Place represents the 18th Century approach to great, landscaped gardens cut out of the tidewater wilderness in 1741 by Henry Middleton, President of the First Continental Congress. Middleton Place was one of the important seats of Revolutionary leadership. After Henry's resignation from the Congress, his son Arthur was elected and became a signer of the Declaration of Independence as was Henry's son-in-law, Edward Rutledge. The elder Middleton is credited with having recruited, equipped and supported an entire regiment in the Revolutionary War.

Middleton Place's well-earned reputation as a hotbed of independence cost it dearly when it was seized and occupied by the British who stripped it of its objects of art, pillaged its storehouses, and despoiled its landscape.

The estate again felt the hot tongue of war when, in 1865, a raiding party put the torch to the magnificent building of more than 300-foot frontage. So complete was the destruction that only the south wing could be restored.

While it is doubtful that Henry Middleton's mansion may ever be rebuilt, his accomplishments as seen in the gardens he designed and constructed on over 60 acres give some measure of this great early American patriot.

The superb terraces leading to the butterfly lakes are an outstanding example of symmetrical balance, order, and elegance designed by man.

The first four camellias in America were planted at Middleton by the French botanist, Andre Michaux. Three of these and a sport of the fourth survive and thrive today.

In 1916, the Middleton descendant, J.J. Pringle Smith, who had inherited the place, began the epic job of restoring the earthquake, war, and neglect-damaged gardens. Even more, Mr. and Mrs. Smith enlarged the gardens, utilizing, as did Henry Middleton, the hills which exist here for maximum display of the colorful blooms. The slopes above the old rice mill pond were heavily planted with the azaleas which flame with dramatic beauty in the Southern spring.

The Smiths' grandson, Charles Duell, is continuing the work by restoring the stableyards, livestock, and plantation work areas to give a more complete picture of a way of life which no longer exists. Sheep graze the great lawn and their presence renews the reason for the ha-ha wall which separates the reflecting pool from the forecourt lawns. Middleton is open the year-round, its plantings of summer, autumn and winter blooms being broadened and increased to keep it beautiful around the calendar. In 1971, Middleton was awarded the State's highest travel award, the Governor's Cup.

Looking down the length of the wall reveals the "ha-ha" moat.

Aerial view of Middleton shows terracing and butterfly lakes to excellent advantage.

Magnolia
Charleston Area

"Magnolia-on-the-Ashley" has continuously been owned by the Drayton family for over two hundred and eighty years. The present owners, C. Norwood Hastie and J. Drayton Hastie, great grandsons of the garden's designer, are the ninth generation of Draytons at Magnolia.

The residence is the third, the first two having been lost to fire. The second was burned by Federal troops. The present house, built during Reconstruction Days, uses the old steps which were the only thing to have survived the Civil War.

The grandson of the first Thomas Drayton had no son to carry on the Drayton name at Magnolia and it was decided that the eldest son of his eldest daughter should change his name of Grimke for that of his grandfather. This son was shot and killed in a deer-hunting accident. His younger brother John was summoned home from his schooling in Europe to take over the Magnolia heritage. He adopted the Drayton name and, as John Grimke-Drayton, became the master of Magnolia. A minister, he developed tuberculosis soon after his ordination in 1851. His physician advised that John must turn to the outdoors and the soil for his principal occupation if he was to have any hope of recovery from his illness. Thus, he began the gardens which now exist at Magnolia.

It would not have been surprising if the Rev. Mr. Grimke-Drayton had followed the same formal paths taken by others—he had himself seen the European gardens' emphasis on sophisticated design. Instead, his acute sensitivity to the spirit of his surroundings which had their own native beauty directed his efforts toward an empathetic harmonizing with indigenous growth and form. The results have been called "other-worldly" by such great writers as John Galsworthy. It is a sad commentary on man's reaction to this natural beauty that he should think of it as "unnatural." It would seem more appropriate to write that Magnolia is "real-worldly."

From the majestic loblolly pines to the magnolias, live oaks, and cypresses wreathed in Spanish moss, banksia, Cherokee rose, jessamine and wisteria overhead—from the atamasco lilies, mosses and ferns to the rhododendrons, pyracantha, hollies, azaleas, and camellias at ground and eye level—everywhere there is the beauty of God. This was the 19th century return to nature.

Great pines soar heavenward above Magnolia's lawns.

Cypress Gardens
Charleston Area

Cypress Gardens' two hundred and fifty acres were once part of the great Dean Hall Plantation on the Cooper River. Like the other plantations of this area, rice was the principal crop, the successful growing of which required abundant sources of fresh water to counteract the brackishness of the tidal flows. The lakes of Cypress Gardens were natural, needing only dykes to impound and control their waters. After the Civil War much of the plantation reverted to wilderness and the water reserves became again a wild forest area.

Benjamin R. Kittredge, the owner of Dean Hall, began in 1927 to reclaim the lakes. His idea was that the brilliant beauty of azalea plantings along the banks would be doubled by the high reflectivity of the placid water turned black by the emission of tannic acid from the myriad cypresses standing offshore.

Two hundred men worked for several years just clearing the lakes of accumulated debris and undergrowth to open the waters to the passage of small boats. Paths and dykes were extended to connect islands to the shore and to lead to the remote recesses of the forest. Thousands of azaleas were set out and tons of narcissus, daffodils, and daphne odora were planted to join the atamasco lilies. They provide a glorious display for shore and water surface, but the real glory of Cypress is the atmosphere created by the great trees standing in the water with their knees breaking the smooth expanse of mirrored quiet.

The visitor who is content with viewing the gardens by foot or who settles for seeing from a boat deprives himself of half the beauty—the Gardens, and the visitor, deserve both views. Each is rewarding in its own way—one for its waterborne serenity and sense of detachment, the other for the intimacy of personal involvement with land and growth.

In 1963, Cypress Gardens was donated to the City of Charleston. The Gardens are now operated under an independent board and the City Council of Charleston.

Of thirty-eight "great gardens of the western world," seven are located in the United States. Of these seven, three are Cypress, Magnolia and Middleton.

The eerie stillness of Cypress is hardly disturbed by a solitary boatman.

Brookgreen Gardens
Murrell's Inlet, S.C.

In 1930, Mr. and Mrs. Archer M. Huntington purchased Brookgreen and its adjoining plantations—The Oaks, Springfield, and Laurel Hill—with the thought of building a winter home as well as a place for displaying Mrs. Huntington's sculpture. From this developed a wider vision of perpetuation of the natural beauty of these thousands of acres while at the same time providing safe haven for the wildlife of the area and a permanent exhibition of American sculpture.

The plan of the garden walks was drawn by Mrs. Huntington. The great garden took the form of a butterfly with outspread wings, all the pathways winding around the central space that was the original plantation homesite. No architect assisted in the plan. Within two years the gardens were so well advanced that they were opened to the public.

To insure the perpetuity of the Gardens, Brookgreen Gardens, a Society for the Southeastern Flora and Fauna, was founded by Mr. Huntington who deeded about 10,000 acres to the corporation and created an endowment fund for its maintenance. A Board of Trustees was appointed to manage the Corporation for the public and implement the aims of the founders as stated by Mr. Huntington: "Brookgreen Gardens is a quiet joining of hands between science and art. The original plan involved a tract of land from the Waccamaw River to the sea in Georgetown County, South Carolina, for the preservation of the flora and fauna of the Southeast. At first the garden was intended to contain the sculpture of Anna Hyatt Huntington. This has gradually found extension in an outline collection representative of the history of American sculpture, from the nineteenth century, which finds its natural setting out of doors. It is not an experiment station nor a research plant. Its object is the presentation of the natural life of a given district as a museum, and as it is a garden, and gardens have from early times been rightly embellished by the art of the sculptor, that principle has found expression in American creative art.

"It is, however, by no means the object of this endeavor to preserve or exhibit objects which have for their only claim to interest their association with names or events or the history of crafts. It is felt that the early culture of the pioneers is most adequately expressed and guarded in old and established museums, leaving to this venture the presenting of the simple forms of nature and of natural beauty together with such artistic works as may express the objects sought.

Wheeler Williams' "Black Panther" stands alert in open ground.

"To these have been added, within the bounds stated, the verse of some of those writers who have taken pleasure in the beauty of nature and her living forms, now so rapidly being depleted through ignorance and greed. In all due homage to science it may be well not to forget inspiration, the sister of religion, without whose union this world might yet become a desert.

"These gardens form the final link in a chain of three wildlife refuges: the first in the Adirondacks in New York consisting of about 16,000 acres of forest and lakes; the second at Newport News, Virginia, devoted to the study of the sea, which, though smaller, reports extraordinary numbers of birds resting there and later continuing their annual flight to Brookgreen, Florida and South America."

Thus was created (at the birthplace of Washington Allston in 1779, an important figure in American painting) a permanent home for representational sculpture and the nature it depicts.

Native wild flowers and plants are featured here. Over five hundred different species and varieties are now growing at Brookgreen.

In addition to the free-moving wildlife which abounds in this refuge, a small zoo is maintained to permit constant observation of the animals by visitors and artists who use them as models.

In 1961, the Trustees leased a large tract—Magnolia Island—a strip of sand beach along the seashore, separated from the mainland by marshes, to the State of South Carolina for recreational purposes. It was named Huntington Beach State Park. The entrance is directly across the road from the entrance to the Gardens.

The administration building at the Gardens is a beautiful, simple structure which unobtrusively takes its place in its surroundings as a quiet complement to them.

The beauty created by sculptors is dramatized and increased by the settings and the play of light and shadow of sun and foliage. The sculpture plays a reciprocal role in providing contrast for the living things whose shadows caress it.

There is one notable paradox in this place which emphasizes the preservation of nature and reverence for life. Much of the sculpture is a restating of classical Greek themes of the hunt and the taming of wild things. While there are some huge, monumental works, the emphasis is on more intimate pieces, natural in scale and subject. As with many art exhibits, it is easy to miss much of the quality and beauty which takes its place so well that it is felt rather than consciously seen. It is well to give enough time to go over and over the Gardens to discover something else with each viewing.

The Gardens are a domain of contemplative solitude as expressed in these lines from the garden:

"Come to the silver gardens of the South,
  Where whisper hath her monarchy, and winds
  Deftly devise live tapestries of shade,
  In glades of stillness patterned . . ."

The hundreds of sculptures displayed throughout the gardens are graced by individual settings and plantings conceived to best express the character of the sculpture they are near.

Mr. James Hagood
Charleston, S.C.

There is a common misconception that the only really good garden is an old garden. Anyone seeing the small townhouse garden of Mr. James Hagood might easily think that it is an old, well-established place which proves the point. This garden, in fact, proves the falsity of the misconception. Its first plants were set in March of 1970. It is so well conceived and executed that it has about it the look and feel of rich maturity. Of course, much of the planting here is not new except to this setting. When the Hagoods moved from Legare Street, it was agreed that Mrs. Hagood could take old flower friends from that garden. Apparently they are happy in their new home.

The house rises from the sidewalk edge on Meeting Street and is separated from its neighbor by a narrow brick-paved drive. These features, while not unattractive in themselves, do not give much opportunity to develop an "atmosphere"; yet, the garden has a magnetic attraction, even for the casual passerby. Like a beautiful veiled woman whose eyes alone can be seen and felt, the garden exudes an air of alluring mystery. Private, proper and innocent it offers hospitality and gregariousness.

What was the magic that brought forth, like Adam or Eve, this loveliness? There was a plot of land 45 x 50 feet with an old brick shed/garage, an old tool shed and two large trees—plus determination, vision, wherewithal, and knowledge. Not everyone can view a block of granite or a piece of wood and see within its exterior surface and dimension all that is necessary for the creation of new beauty. The magic is the alchemy of art which can transform raw materials into thoroughly realized form and texture and color. The gardener is artist, tool, and medium working in collaboration with the ultimate artist, nature.

Brick and flagstone paving accentuate form and make for easy maintenance.

An open gate makes a double statement of privacy and of welcome.

In this garden there were two human artists in collaboration: Mrs. Hagood, a former garden club president, and Mr. Loutrel Briggs, a noted landscape architect and horticulturist.

The garage and the tool shed were taken down and the brick saved. One tree was removed to open the way for additional sunlight. The ground was cleared and sculpted into terraces. Walls and walks were built and paved with the brick from the demolished structures. Flagstone was brought in to complete the surfacing of the unplanted areas—after piping to the fountains was laid. A small, garden sitting room with attached greenhouse was built of the remainder of the salvaged brick. The plantings were set, and a garden came into being.

The specific ingredients above are important and can easily be listed, but the unseen necessities for producing a great result are not so easy to describe. The elements of experience, imagination, patience, love, genius and good taste, which are a part of this garden, are there but cannot be dissected and dispassionately laid out for viewing. They are just there as the soul of the garden, as the soul of nature itself.

The French doors of the sitting room allow for a wide open relationship with the garden itself—a relationship which is heightened by the rough shaped stone reciprocating fountain which plays water down the rock onto maidenhair fern.

Jenkins Mikell House
94 Rutledge Ave., Charleston, S.C.

At the corner of Rutledge Avenue and Montague Street in Charleston stands the Mikell House, a great antebellum townhouse mansion (one of the last in Charleston) built by Jenkins Mikell in 1853 for his bride. As the owner of vast plantations on Edisto Island, he made a fortune growing sea island cotton.

The house was built in the grandiose manner of an Italian Villa. The south portico is as magnificent as any in the South. The exterior is entirely in the ochre color characteristic of Italian buildings of that period. Unique in Charleston are its Jupiter or ram's head capitals on the great Corinthian columns which are each of one solid piece of wood, carved to match the others.

After several changes of ownership, the property was purchased by the County of Charleston and from 1936 to 1960 housed the County library. The removal of the library to Marion Square made possible the purchase of the property in 1962 by Mr. and Mrs. Charles H. Woodward. They were the only ones to bid since it was feared that much expensive reconstruction would be necessary to effect complete restoration. Only one sill needed replacement, so well was the building constructed and preserved. House and gardens are beautifully maintained.

Mr. Loutrel Briggs designed the major portion of the present gardens. The area along Rutledge Avenue contains what remains of the original garden planting and design. The walkways are of crushed pink-red brick fragments whose color is in perfect harmony with the ochre color of the mansion, the greens of the garden, and the tanbark mulch.

The entire property is enclosed by perforated walls and wrought-iron fences which permit pleasurable viewing of the house and garden from the outside. Wrought-iron grillwork of great artistry is one of the features of old Charleston. Its design and character heighten the charm of the old buildings and the walls and the gardens of this lovely city, which shows so much interest in preserving what is best of its colorful past.

Loutrel Briggs restoration recaptures flavor of original gardens.

View from upper level of mansion shows garden, perforated wall, columns, and flooring of gallery.

Mr. and Mrs. Robert Whitelaw
42 State Street, Charleston, S.C.

This garden is only a few years old but it and the house and area around it are full of history. This was a part of "old Charleston" which was going down in the familiar pattern of urban deterioration. Forty-two State Street was the first reclamation of an old house in its immediate area. Now, the entire street has benefitted from similar restoration. This is an example of what can be done by industrious devotion to the preservation of beauty within city confines.

The house was built by a shipwright in 1813. It later became a coffee storage warehouse. The coffee mill grindstone set in the driveway is not only attractive but serves as a reminder of the use to which the building was put before rehabilitation.

All of the present exterior beauty is the accomplishment in design, execution, and maintenance of the present owners, Mr. and Mrs. Robert Whitelaw.

The walls and paving of the garden and porch were built and laid of brick made by Mr. Whitelaw according to the old Charleston formula—hand molded, sun dried, and fired in a wood-burning kiln.

The design of the wall leading into the garden is copied from the Morley Williams design created for Tryon Palace in New Bern, North Carolina.

A perforated, ventilated wall hides from the street the evidence of the existence of the porch while allowing a view from the inside to the street.

A balustraded wall separates the garden from the laundry yard and tool storage area. The balustrades permit maximum air movement in and to the garden. The balustrades themselves were rescued from the demolition of another old Charleston house.

The back wall, with its charming built-in arch, is part of a warehouse in which Mr.

Whitelaw now has a workshop studio where he constructs dioramas for museums.

Behind the laundry yard is a former alley, now privately owned, which once housed a row of taverns in one of which was established the first Masonic Lodge in Charleston. This gave the name of Lodge Alley to the street.

17th Century Japanese Buddha before which Mr. Whitelaw's daughter was married by a Presbyterian minister.

The ivy covered wall of the garden is not really a wall but a low cyclone fence to both sides of which Mr. Whitelaw lashed native bamboo strips, keeping their bases a few inches above ground level to prevent deterioration. This device has proved successful since the bamboo has withstood twelve years of exposure without any harm.

The garden itself is low maintenance in both cost and time. Most of the flowers other than the camellias and azaleas which are an integral part of the planting are potted plants set on the brick step around the fountain.

A small courtyard between the porch and the garden was hand excavated and paved with Mr. Whitelaw's brick.

The garden level is the same as that of the porch.

At the back, framed by planting, with the background of the arch in the brick wall, is a stone 17th century Japanese Buddha before which the Whitelaw's daughter was married by a Presbyterian minister in the summer of 1965.

In old Charleston, with the bustle of the city all around it, State Street is a place of tranquil geniality which demonstrates anew how people can live graciously in close proximity with their neighbors while preserving the history and tradition of the past.

The terracing and fountain installation are all the work of the Whitelaws.

Car park and garden gate as seen from the street. The perforations in the brick wall allow for ventilation and outward viewing from the screened porch.

Heyward-Washington House
87 Church St., Charleston, S.C.

This fine old "double" house was built in 1770 by Daniel Heyward. His son, Thomas Heyward, Jr., who lived here, was a delegate to the Continental Congress and a signer of the Declaration of Independence for South Carolina.

In May of 1791, President George Washington was lodged in the Heyward House for an extended period of time. From the staircase and bedroom windows he would, as an avid gardener himself, certainly have admired the formal garden set behind the Kitchen and Carriage Houses.

From its earliest days in 1682, Charleston has always been garden conscious. Thomas Ash wrote then that, while heretofore they (the Carolinians) had been engaged in settling their plantations, "now their gardens begin to be supplied with such European Plants and Herbs as are necessary for the Kitchen, viz. Potatoes, Lettice, Colesworts, Parsnip, Carrot and Reddish: their gardens also begin to be beautified and adorned with such Herbs and Flowers which to the Smell or Eye are pleasing and agreeable, viz. the Rose, Carnation and Lilly, &c."

It is certain that Mr. Heyward's fine townhouse was blessed with such a garden. Time and change of living patterns took their toll of both house and plantings, and restoration was necessary to bring both back to full beauty.

In 1931, the Heyward-Washington House, as it had become known, had been partially restored and opened to visitors but the garden was still covered with concrete and the rubble of broken bricks. There was no record of the old garden design or planting. It was necessary to reconstruct what might have been.

The actual work, after the rubble had been removed, was begun and the garden laid out by the designer with the help of a yardstick, a piece of string, and a young black lad. Many friends generously gave old-fashioned plants from their own gardens, while others made gifts of money with which to buy additional plants.

It was decided not to plant anything in this garden which had been introduced into cultivation after the date of Washington's stay in 1791. It was necessary to determine positively what plants qualified. Great care was taken to determine that "native" plants which might have been used are really "natives" and not escapes of a later date.

One of the sources of identification were the advertisements which appeared in old newspapers such as the South Carolina Gazette in whose issue of December 23-30, 1732, Samuel Everleigh offered for sale "divers sorts of best Garden seeds." Orange, lime and lemon trees were often advertised for sale and shown as flourishing on properties offered for sale. It would appear from this that the climate was somewhat warmer in those days than at present.

From the window of the bedroom occupied by General Washington, the garden's pattern may be seen.

The pre-Revolution garden tool shed and kitchen still stand.

The advertisements and articles which appeared in London gazettes of that period were also studied since they gave evidence that seeds, trees and shrubs of indigenous Carolina growth were exported to England to "enrich that country's growth."

The 1841 edition of *Loudon's Encyclopedia of plants* lists plants native to or grown in England with the dates the plants were introduced to England and the places of origin. This demonstrates the authenticity of native American plants which were dated before the possibility of escapes might have occurred. It was felt that the continuous intercourse between Charleston and England would have made quite certain that the plants from other areas of the world would have been introduced to Charleston about the same time.

The rectangular garden of the Heyward House is centered by a circular pattern which is repeated in each of the five-bedded quadrants. Along the back is a bed which contains ground cover and flowering shrubs.

Such gardens as this provided a bit of formal horticultural sophistication within severe space limitations behind the townhouses of the plantation owners such as Mr. Heyward. They required less upkeep and attention than the extensive plantation gardens. Like old friends, these small gardens seem to say, "Come, grow old along with me, I will give you so much and ask from you so little more than your love."

Facade of the Heyward-Washington House.

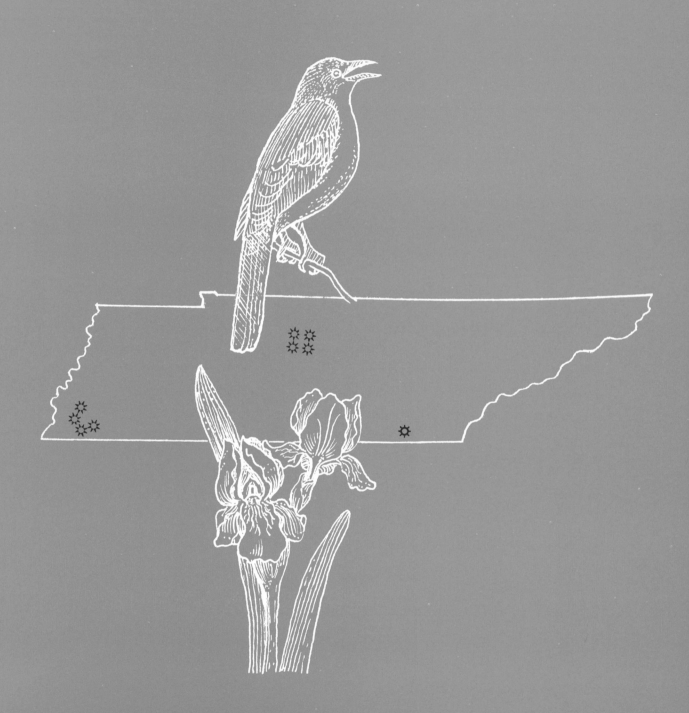

TENNESSEE

Rock City Gardens
Lookout Mountain,
Chattanooga, Tennessee

Whether swathed in moist, downy clouds which intensify concentration on close-up things which can still be seen through the mist or bathed in warm sun on a clear day which permits full enjoyment of the beauty of its panoramas, Rock City is a natural phenomenon set high in the sky.

In 1924, Mr. and Mrs. Garnet Carter bought ten acres of this stone cliffside and built, at the great overlook, their home. Mrs. Carter and a friend walked the land seeking out the natural paths through fissures and over narrow chasms. As they roamed the rock they marked the paths with twine they carried for the purpose. Then she set out to plant the area with all the plant life native to the site. But to plant meant first to bring in earth to cover inhospitable rock sculptured through eons of time by wind, water and upthrust of earth's crust.

The work that was done gives a home for over four hundred varieties of Tennessee and Georgia uplands flora enhanced by plantings of bulbs and alpines whose native homes are similar to their new location. All of this greenery and blossom is in such contrast to the stark drama of the rock formations that each heightens the effect of the other.

The result of Mrs. Carter's efforts won for her the Garden Club of America Bronze Medal of Distinction for outstanding achievement in horticulture and conservation.

In addition to nature's handiwork with stone, there are paths and bridges and guard walls and buildings, all the work of men. Stone masonry, a vanishing art in most places, still flourishes here through the natural tendency of the Lookout Mountain-folk to hand down from generation to generation the crafts of the family. Rock City gives continuing employment to the services of these hardy individualists.

The history of the ages is written here—on the rocks where the imprint of sea fossils tells us that this mountaintop was once ocean bed, and in the stonework of the age of man, the builder.

The garden is a constantly evolving thing whose pathways are changed to accommodate the desires of visitors. When people habitually leave walkways in specific areas to better view some growth or scene, instead of insisting on strict use of the walk, the walk location is changed. The director of the gardens has said, "People who travel feel a lack of familiar places, friends, and things. Rock City is a place where the traveler may stop to reestablish his association with nature to fill this void."

Mrs. Carter made a garden place of beauty in the sky as a work of love. She was enabled to do this because her husband was a

The residence at Rock City looks out from the edge of the mountain top.

successful entrepreneur who had capitalized on his development and franchising of miniature golf. He sold his interests and invested his returns only to be hard hit in the stock market crash of 1929. With his promotional ability it was natural for him to make of the gardens an "attraction." Because he was so successful in his promotional efforts, the gardens are seen each year by 600,000 people. It is all to the good that, for whatever reason, so many people are brought into direct contact with Mrs. Carter's garden built on nature's grandeur. She would certainly have been pleased to know that so many have enjoyed her work. It is not so certain that she would have been happy with the hundreds of miles of highways and waysides degraded by billboards and barn signs advertising Rock City and its competing attractions on Lookout Mountain. New, less offensive means of calling drivers' attention to Rock City are being investigated and planned. One of these is the possibility of controlled roadway radio signal advertising. This would be an improvement since sound is transitory and the radio signal would be subject to the choice of the listener.

At Rock City Gardens, natural rock surface forms and floral beauty are given a feel of life over life by streams and the five dramatic waterfalls which run with water pumped up to the garden height from the valley so far below.

Delicate blossoms flutter in the mountain breeze against a background of rock mountainside and distant land and sky. Long after the undesirable aspects of commercialism will have passed away, Mrs. Carter's work will remain as a welcome addition to nature's work. The trees and shrubs and flowers will propagate themselves and be spread by wind and bird to multiply the beauty brought here by Mrs. Carter, musician, artist and gardener. Time may erase the far-flung negatives while carrying farther afield to every hospitable place the seeds of loveliness set on a foundation of solid stone.

The swinging bridge is 180 feet long and 80 feet above a rock valley.

Middleton, South Carolina

Rock City, Tennessee

Hermitage and Travellers' Rest, Tennessee

Middleton, South Carolina

Rock City, Tennessee

Magnolia, South Carolina

Cypress, South Carolina

The grand corridor is the introduction to the garden.

The Hermitage and Travellers' Rest

Nashville, Tennessee

On 625 hilly acres of Middle Tennessee about twelve miles from Nashville is Andrew Jackson's home, The Hermitage. He bought the land in 1804, sixteen years after he came to Nashville.

The first structures at The Hermitage were log buildings as sturdy as Jackson himself. They were built close together, the largest being a two-story blockhouse constructed to resist possible Indian attacks. Humble as they were, the smaller cabins accommodated such guests as Aaron Burr, President James Monroe and the then young Jefferson Davis.

After General Jackson had achieved national renown as the hero of New Orleans and the Florida Campaign of 1818, he and his wife Rachel began to build a residence she felt was more suitable to a national hero. The first Hermitage was their happy home until Rachel's death in 1828 just before his inaugural as President of the United States.

Andrew Jackson had married Rachel Robards in 1791 in Natchez, Mississippi. Unknown to them at the time, her first husband had not pursued the petition granted him by the Virginia Assembly permitting him to seek a divorce from Rachel in court. In 1794, Andrew and Rachel Jackson were married a second time. It was a successful marriage but the charges made against Rachel by her first husband and the subsequent shadow cast on her relationship with Jackson haunted them both for the remainder of her life.

Four years after Rachel's death, the roof of the house caught fire and in a few hours almost the entire structure was destroyed. The indomitable Jackson had it rebuilt, using as much of the original brick and wood as could be salvaged.

To the east of the mansion is the garden which Jackson had laid out for his beloved Rachel. It was designed by William Frost, an English landscapist of Philadelphia. It is a square of over an acre in size, quadrated around a circular flower garden. The outer quadrants were used for the cultivation of kitchen vegetables. The garden was a prime interest in Rachel Jackson's daily life. The age of the garden is indicated by the moss which grows on the old brick bedding edges.

The old oaken bucket is a reality at the Hermitage.

During his two terms as President, Jackson found difficulty in obtaining an overseer who would satisfactorily maintain "Rachel's Garden." When this problem was finally overcome he wrote his son, "How I am delighted to hear that the garden has regained its former appearance that it always possessed when your dear mother was living, and that just attention is now paid to her monument. This is truly pleasing to hear, and precisely as it ought to be."

During the Civil War a guard of Federal troops was sent out from Nashville to protect the Hermitage. The garden, enclosed as it was by a fence, made a convenient corral for the military's horses and the garden was almost obliterated in the three years the guard was stationed here.

Today, the garden lies just about as it was during Rachel's time. The moss-covered brick borders have withstood the ravages of misuse and time so there was little difficulty in determining the exact shapes and locations of the beds. The weeding and clearing which preceded the replanting of the restoration was not so easy, but perseverance has produced an end result that is a faithful re-creation of the original, containing 44 varieties of plants, shrubs and trees.

The focal highlight is the tomb located in the southeast corner of the garden. The tomb and the burying ground adjacent to it were established by President Jackson when Rachel died. Great magnolias watch over the area as do the shagbark hickories next to the man lovingly known to his soldiers and countrymen as "Old Hickory." The simple garden of a rugged man, it has shown the same strength and spirit of survival that marked its founder.

Judge John Overton, a lifelong friend and law partner of Andrew Jackson, managed Jackson's political campaigns. A well-rounded man of many activities, Overton was a pioneer, one of the founders of Memphis, a horticulturist, a politician, a

Travellers' Rest is an unpretentious garden of old-fashioned, simple charm.

In the far corner of the garden the Jackson tomb stands alongside the family cemetery.

Buildings of the original Hermitage are a far cry from the loveliness of Jackson's mansion.

public servant, an educator, Master Mason, Jurist and Statesman.

He acquired the land for his plantation in 1796 and began building the residence two years later. Successive generations of Overton descendants occupied the house until 1946 when it was purchased by the Louisville and Nashville Railroad. Through the urging of the Colonial Dames of America in Tennessee, the railroad deeded the property to that organization for restoration and preservation as a historical museum. It is an appropriate companion to the Hermitage since the founders of both places were such close friends and associates.

These gardens are relatively small and simple but possess a charm altogether in keeping with the house and setting. The dominant plantings are yucca, ivy and boxwood which combine so well with the magnolias and hollies. The low brick wall sets the formal garden off without interfering with its relationship to the house. The size and character of the garden, like the house, are similar to the Hermitage in that they accurately reflect sturdy men and women of pioneering strength whose major ties were more with simplicity than with opulent design or ostentation. Rachel Jackson, Mrs. Overton and Mrs. Cheek were all enthusiastic gardeners and, like gardeners everywhere, exchanged slips and cuttings of their best plants. There were, then, blood, or sap, ties as well as friendship between Hermitage's and Travellers' gardens.

Six great columns grace the front entry to the Hermitage.

Cheekwood
Nashville, Tennessee

The construction of Cheekwood was begun as a private estate in 1929 by Mr. and Mrs. Leslie Cheek. The exterior is faced with limestone quarried from the spot on which the huge mansion stands. Some of the architectural motifs were fashioned from this rock and most of the rock in the gardens comes from the same source.

In 1957 it was offered by the Walter Sharps who had inherited it as a gift to a non-profit organization created to maintain Cheekwood as a cultural center.

The house is used as a museum; art gallery; art reference library; concert, film and lecture center; and art school. Offices for the administration of the Botanical Gardens have recently been moved to the new Botanic Hall.

The two directors, one for the Arts and one for the Botanical Gardens, cooperate in selecting the outdoor sculpture and decorative garden pieces and the indoor floral decoration.

The gardens are regarded as not only a place for growing things but as a growing place, constantly evolving and changing. The director, P. Duncan Callicott, courageously has pruned, trimmed and removed plants which have outgrown their settings. He functions in the same way and with the same freedom that a good private gardener does, changing, developing and improving the various areas of the gardens to improve views and to make maximum use of space and vista.

When the famous Nashville garden, Wildings, was given to Cheekwood it was moved in large pieces, rocks, plants and soil, from the old Howe home to a location at the Botanical Gardens to be called the Wildings section.

A new Botanical building is nearing completion. It will enlarge the community service programs of instruction in landscape design, nature study, horticulture, botany and related subjects; the cultivation of the best native and exotic plant material to which Nashville is hospitable; and the presentation of flower shows and exhibits throughout the year. The new building's terrace is so planned that its mass plantings will themselves provide constant flower shows. There are additional educational projects such as merit badge courses in conservation for Girl and Boy Scouts.

Display beds are maintained in the gardens by the Middle Tennessee Daffodil, Hemerocallis and Iris Societies. Effective use is made of flowing and impounded water through fountains, ripple falls and water lily reflection pools.

Ripple falls bubble and gurgle down the rocky slopes.

One of the unusual displays which is an annual feature that attracts thousands of children and adults is the Christmas Trees of Many Lands Show whose earnings are used to further garden projects.

The hospitality symbol, a pineapple, is widely used at Cheekwood in stone and metalwork. It has been adopted as the visual symbol for Cheekwood. It could well serve for all of Nashville which exudes welcome and friendliness.

Under construction is the Tritchler Memorial Garden which will house 478 species of shrubs which the local nurserymen consider acclimated to Middle Tennessee.

The estate contains one of the major boxwood gardens in the United States.

Though there is a professional staff at the gardens, there is plenty of opportunity for volunteers to become directly involved, not only as guides but in the weeding that is a constant chore in such a large area of cultivated growth.

An enrichment botany course is under the joint sponsorship of the Botanical Gardens and the Junior League of Nashville, for the fifth grade students of the Metropolitan school system. The program consists of four slide lectures given in the school classrooms and a field trip to the nature trails at Cheekwood.

Cheekwood is a place for all the people of the Nashville area, to view and to study and to participate in the creation and enjoyment of beauty, natural and man-made.

Middle Tennessee's hills call for the development of terraces.

The formal magnificence of the mansion is tempered by the informality of ground plantings.

Raajel
Belle Meade, Tennessee

Not far from Cheekwood and old Belle Meade Mansion is the Rufus Fort, Jr., home —Raajel. It sits on an elevation with a wide lawn around it and a large stream below. The drive is straight and broad to a forecourt beautifully planted with evergreens. Some hug the ground, some rise just above it, and some stand in restrained majesty to frame statuary and cover walls. Boxwood and wisteria play an important part in most Nashville gardens, but Mrs. Fort has chosen not to make extensive use of either, preferring the varied forms and textures of her planting to set off and dramatize the reflecting pool, the loggia, and the house. An ivy covered wall parallels the ell of the house to complete the enclosure of the forecourt and leads to a patio beyond graceful, white-painted wrought-iron gates.

The ground slopes away from the patio to a stone-stepped overlook above the broad stream which has cut away the ledge rock whose outcroppings make a natural rock garden in which small wild flowers abound.

Around the house, to the right, are iron-fenced terraces which display notable garden sculptures to maximum advantage. The terraces continue around the house above the wide lawns which house a wrought-iron pergola ensconced in heavy planting and a set of children's swings. Plastic balls and toy automobiles, instead of striking a disharmonious note in this impeccably groomed garden, are a warm reminder that youngsters are being indoctrinated to well-maintained beauty by being allowed freely to play and enjoy these grounds.

Wrought-iron pattern of patio gates continues around the patio and side and back terraces.

Below the pergola, the slope is covered with rock garden plantings that are an intermediate step between the formality of the upper level and the natural growth on the banks of the brook that runs at right angles to and feeds the main stream—Richland Creek.

Unmistakably, Raajel is an estate meticulously groomed and carefully planted to make maximum use of land contours and to emphasize the architecture of the house; but its effect is one of cooperation with nature as it gives itself to nature as a foreground or a backdrop just as it uses nature for similar purposes. It is a fair exchange.

While Raajel obviously is a garden beyond the means of the average person, it is also a demonstration of restraint which permits no ostentation or showiness. As it is without flamboyance, it is rich with quiet self-assurance.

The painted brick of the house is not ivy-grown as are the garden walls. The ivy, ground cover or climbing, gives a background and underbacking for a variety of hollies and deciduous shrubs. Color is used sparingly. Blossoms do not have to compete for attention with other blossoms. They are allowed to brighten the garden with soft whispers rather than strident shouts.

Mrs. Fort is as unassuming and as strong as the gardens whose charm so accurately reflects the mistress. That grandchildren and their toys have the run of the lovely grounds says more for Mrs. Fort's gracious humanity than any other single thing could do.

Side terrace looks out over Richland Creek.

Tributary to Richland Creek is the center of interest in the nature area.

Memphis Botanic Garden
Memphis, Tennessee

Memphis is a city in the forefront of urban public recognition of ecological problems and the necessity for expanding open land areas even within municipal boundaries. As a medium-size metropolitan area, Memphis also is a leader in the amount of its space devoted to parkland. There are over 5000 acres in existing city parks plus the county parks under the authority of the Parks Commission. Additional land is being acquired to enlarge this acreage.

The Botanic Garden is staffed and maintained by the Park Commission. It was only in November of 1970 that the entire facility was chartered, but the Ketchum Memorial Iris Garden, occupying five and one-half acres, was given to the city in 1953. The specially designated Committee of the Memphis Area Iris Society has, throughout the years, planted, maintained and improved the Iris Garden which contains over 800 outstanding varieties that bloom over a period of about six weeks each year.

The W. C. Paul Arboretum was established in Audubon Park in 1957 and four years later the extensive Wild Flower Garden and Magnolia Garden were begun. The Arboretum contains many domestic and foreign shrubs and at least one tree of every commercial species known. The Magnolia Garden with 80 varieties is said to be the largest of its kind. The Wild Flower Garden covers a large area adjacent to the Japanese Garden, designed by Dr. Tono of Japan, which is now being developed. The Japanese bridge and walks and lake have been completed and the lake is stocked with 5000 goldfish. This work is being done with the cooperation of the Memphis Chapter of Ikebana International.

The daffodil collection has something over 500 varieties. The rose garden is made up of 3000 bushes of many colors and varieties. The Ruth Norfleet Camellia Lath House was given by the Norfleet family and contains their collection of fine old plants. Judge

Andrew O. Holmes Greenhouse will feature the study and exhibition of camellias grown under glass. The azalea trail concentrates this species' brilliance in one large area which does not compete with the more subtle colors of other blooms.

All of the garden areas mentioned above are the results of gifts which, by their size and number, tell their own story of love of flowers and the civic interests of Memphis families and organizations.

Yet to be mentioned is the Goldsmith Civic Garden Center presented to the people of Memphis by the Goldsmith Family in memory of Jacob Goldsmith. In seeking a fitting memorial the family decided that, because Memphis is flower-minded and is fortunate in being able to grow an unusually large variety of flowers, plants and shrubs, a Civic Garden Facility would be most appropriate and useful. In 1964, the Center was dedicated. "The value of a public institution depends on the use that people make of it. The Goldsmith Civic Garden Center has been established for the enjoyment it will give, and the educational help it will render the people of Memphis and the Mid-South. The Goldsmith family

Sign in the wild flower garden.

Man-made islands will be part of the Oriental Garden which will not stop at the waterline.

will consider the Center a truly fitting memorial only to the extent it plays a living, vital role in the life of our community by increasing the love for gardening, not only among men and women, but also among the boys and girls in school who will be the home gardeners of the future. The Center is here to help all of us learn and discover ways of improving and beautifying our gardens so that the beauty of the gardens in Memphis and the Mid-South will continue to be a source of pleasure for all who view them.'' These are words of a statement of intent and purpose.

Garden clubs take part in the activities of the Center. One of the most active is the Memphis Garden Club, which is responsible for the planting of the entrance, the large glass house, the fountain court and the sculpture court.

Through a window wall of the Center the fountain court or water garden may be seen to good advantage. Designed by William Hager, it is oriental in character with fountains playing water into the reflecting pool bordered by hollies and other evergreens backed by weathered, gray vertical boards. At the far end is a view of the conservatory which may be entered through the walks which flank the water garden.

Japanese garden bench sits above the Oriental
Garden now being built. Water flow feeding the lake
has been cut off while work on the garden progresses.

The sculpture court will display contemporary outdoor art objects.

The conservatory is lush with tropical growth that contrasts with the simplicity of the water garden planting and that of the outdoor sculpture court garden.

The rose garden's thousands of bushes are laid out in an intricate geometric pattern within a square, double quadrated by diagonals and bisectors, and three circles within circles.

The character of the fountain court and the developing Japanese Garden by the Ikebana Chapter call attention to the history of Memphis interest in Japanese garden design and planting. The large Overton Park did have in it a notable Japanese Garden which was deliberately obliterated and planted over during World War II as an expression of response to the attack on Pearl Harbor. But love has outlasted hate and fury and there is again a strong support for the re-creation of another public Japanese Garden in the Botanic Center. (Some of the accompaning pictures show the work in progress.)

The Memphis area supports 1500 Garden Clubs of which 300 meet in the Center. This incredible number is indicative of the great interest Memphis sustains in matters horticultural. The privately maintained gardens of Memphis give evidence that the interest is not just academic or social. When supermarket fronts and gas stations are graced with good plantings something is right with the city.

The conservatory contains a full variety of tropical plants.

Mr. and Mrs. J.S. Buxton
Memphis, Tennessee

The Buxton property is located on a corner lot in Memphis where the two streets come together at an acute angle. The house parallels the street facing out on a golf course and the entry drive is from the street whose angle creates an asymmetrical situation on all sides.

The initial problem which faced William Hager, the landscape architect, was to work out a design which would create an illusion of regularity without unusual angulation. The entry drive and courtyard perform this function with surprising success. At both sides of the drive entry are examples of one of Mr. Hager's specialties—specially built lanterns of his own design. These are given a surrounding base of white azaleas. The low walls and the terraces are of carefully chosen old brick whose color matches that of the tile roofing of the house. The large courtyard is enclosed by willow leaf holly which is allowed to grow untrimmed. The front terrace was designed to set the house on a horizontal base and provide a transition from the deep, sloping front lawn.

The private rear garden was developed on two levels. The lower terrace next to the house makes for a series of areas whose intimacy is increased by the plantings such as the espaliered fruit trees that give texture and interest to one unwindowed wall. Sidewall and house enclose three sides of the sitting terrace where planting areas and paving work together like the design of a rug to give a unity to the interesting whole. Square stepping-stone walks relieve the regularity of paved paths in the lower terrace without disturbing the flow of line their arrangement achieves.

The upper level adapts to natural grade differences and sets off the fine zoysia lawn of this large area. At the rear and the side is a brick wall brought into harmony with the overall by a paving which repeats the theme established in the entrance court. The wooden screen walls were designed to complete the enclosure and continue the design of the lattice screens of the carport. These walls also serve to set off three small areas, each of which has its own specific purpose: one is the rose garden; one is a wild flower garden; the third is a work and storage area containing the compost heap where leaves and other organic matter are converted to humus.

Plantings and walls were planned to set off, by their colors, the pale ochre of the house. Doors, trim and wood lanterns and wall screens are all of deep chocolate brown. The depth of the holly greens gives them strong definition against house and brick terrace walls.

Most such gardens need meticulous grooming and make no provision for children and large dogs, but this is a garden for total living which happily accommodates both. It is a joyous garden with room for children's play and laughter and for adult relaxation and quiet.

The upper terrace is a fine Zoysia lawn bordered by walls and rich plantings.

135

Mr. and Mrs. W. Jeter Eason
Memphis, Tennessee

The Eason residence gardens look like the product of professional design and planting but they are entirely the work of this talented couple. He is a noted architect and she is an avid gardener, a prominent member of the Memphis Ikebana Chapter.

The Eason's have business interests in the Pacific and are frequent visitors to the Far East. Their home and gardens are showplaces for their important collection of occidental and oriental art.

A system of concealed lighting in the garden subtly illuminates plantings and objects of art. In no case is the light source evident to disturb the focus of eyes adjusted to the darkness of night and in no case does the light cause what might be called a shout of brightness. It is always controlled to be more a whisper of understatement in keeping with the subtleties of the garden itself.

The garden has been conceived and developed for maximum ease of maintenance with brick edging set in to eliminate the edge cutting chore. Azaleas are backed by taller camellias so that the spring blooms of the azalea may have a background of camellia greenery and the autumn and winter-blooming camellias may have a base of azalea foliage.

An intimate garden is contained in a sunken terrace where the feature planting is of *Ilex latifolia.* Cryptomeria used as a screening is the largest in the Memphis area. The screening wall is made up of unusual square and oval shafts of Japanese bamboo which has a long outdoor life.

The small porch, called the "moon gazing platform," is used to good advantage in the daylight hours to display Mrs. Eason's miniaturized trees (bonsai). A marvelously intricate and detailed bas relief carving of teak decorates one wall. The hanging, overhead lights are screened by American designed and manufactured fixtures which look like Japanese origami paper sculpture.

The steps to the garden from the porch are a necessity which violates the Japanese tradition of eliminating stairs to a home entry but Mr. Eason designed this to be as close as possible to the Japanese. It could be called a stile in the Japanese style.

A black stone statue of Kuan-Yin, the Chinese Goddess of Mercy is framed by a planting of Cleyera Japonica and at night is lighted by an unusual lamp designed and fabricated by Mr. Eason. On its face is the Chinese character which means "good fortune." Along the fence behind this stretch is a row of yaupon holly trimmed in cloud shapes.

Eight inch high red deer "go to water" in a miniature mountain setting.

Garden entry hints at the beauty beyond.

In the remote corner is the wild garden which features ferns and mosses. On the wall is a cast-aluminum sculpture and on one of the rocks sits a stylized marble sculpture of a cricket done by a young Chinese-American Memphian.

A hemlock hedge screening is used to frame a "surprise" area, the miniature dry-stream Japanese garden whose crushed-stone base represents water. Two sizes of stone are used, the larger symbolizing deeper water. Rock unusual to this area is artfully arranged to give the impression of tiny mountains against which a pair of red deer of about 8 inches in height are beautifully displayed. A large stone lantern from Kyoto is placed so that its size does not impose itself on the miniaturization nearby.

From the large windows of the dining room is seen a long, narrow garden containing a tapered length of reflecting pool whose wider end is nearer the house. This design serves a double purpose. It gives the pool a more interesting form than it would have had as a rectilinear shape and its taper exaggerates the perspective to create an illusion of great length. At the house end of the pool is a contemporary bronze sculpture of stylized surf-riders. Despite its size, it captures the feeling of buoyancy and movement associated with this sport. The sides of the pool are enclosed by Chinese holly, one side hedged and the other side espaliered.

The cutting garden is situated at the front where its blooms may be enjoyed by neighbors and passersby. In the small greenhouse that is a part of this section, Mrs. Eason has an outstanding collection of camellias and orchids.

Contemporary sculpture finds a place at the reflecting pool.

"Cricket" is a contemporary Oriental-American work.

Gardens of Mr. J.L. Kirkpatrick
Memphis, Tennessee

Only fifteen years ago this lush, mature garden was open meadow land where only a few trees stood. The truth of this is strong testimony to what can be done in a short time.

Mr. Kirkpatrick had studied oriental art in college and had started his substantial collection of Far East art before he began his garden. From this background and association with the Memphis Ikebana group came the inspiration for these gardens. Mr. Kirkpatrick's affinity and desire for the restful, informal quality of the lifestyle suggested and supported by a Japanese home and garden atmosphere are well served inside and out.

The old, Japanese art objects are authentic. They add greatly to the overall atmosphere and to the detail of the several areas. Mr. Kirkpatrick, through the use of a contemporary sculpture near the guest house, has shown that discriminating, good taste in choice and arrangement can result in harmonious relationships between objects of the past and present and East and West.

The guesthouse, across the pool from the main house, won the AID award in 1968 for its architecture and its relationship to its surroundings.

This is a constantly evolving garden whose owner recognizes that much of a garden's continuing beauty depends on subtraction and simplification to give greater emphasis to small or slower growing plants which may be dwarfed by faster growing varieties. He feels that gardeners have a natural tendency to acquire and fill needs too rapidly and that this can only be corrected by the excision of superfluous plantings.

House and garden are inseparable and give to each other not just on the outside but to and from the interior so that an inclement January day, rather than causing a hiatus of enjoyment, brings out facets of the house and garden beauty which are not felt or seen on warm, sunny days. It is like the cheery glow of a fireplace which is never so appreciated as on a dank day.

The totality of success achieved by this marriage of house and garden is the result of a team effort between architect, landscapist and owner. The first two are the media through which the personality and the interests of the last are reflected and come alive in a tangible being. Architect David McGhee and landscape architect William Hager worked together with each other and with the owner in a harmony that lives on and on in their creation.

Mr. Hager's participation goes far beyond basic design of earth contour, level and planting. He designed the lovely, hexagonal teahouse. He designs walls, fences, outdoor lighting, gates, screens, paving motifs and pools.

Hager, like all first-rate professionals and amateurs, benefits from the work of others as well as from his own experience. It is a good lesson for the novice to remember that his own imagination may be stimulated by exposure to the work of others. Hager says, "Even the professional landscape architect derives inspiration and creative ideas from the great gardens others have created before him." This is what artists in many fields do without sacrifice of their individuality or integrity.

This description began with words about the scarcity of trees here before the garden was made. Two large cryptomeria were here and they stand now at the entry whose sweeping form their presence dictated.

This is the home of a gentleman and a gentle man whose quiet charm it so beautifully expresses.

The teahouse completes the garden statement like the signature to a love letter.

MISSISSIPPI

D'Evereux
Natchez, Mississippi

Like others in Natchez, this grand house is a magnificent example of Greek Revival Architecture. Porticos are the full, tall two stories in height. The white of the painted, plastered brick behind and against greenery and blue sky dramatizes the building's purity of line and mass. The metal roof is a soft coral color which caps the house beautifully. At night floodlights dramatically display D'Evereux so that passersby may enjoy its noble façade night or day. The house is owned by two generations of Buckles, T.B., Sr. and Jr. They welcome casual visitors to the garden.

The previous owner was a schoolteacher who moved here on her retirement. It was her intention to plant in these gardens at least one of everything that grows in Mississippi. Though very limited in her financial means, she left Natchez a rich heritage of planted beauty. Miss Myra Smith not only kept D'Evereux Hall going but added to its glory.

During the winter months camellias bloom profusely as do the narcissi. A casual viewer might easily get the impression that the grounds are a little neglected because the lack of meticulous manicuring and barbering is in sharp contrast to the pristine whiteness of the house. It would be a false impression —these gardens are meant to reflect natural growth rather than a tailored quality. From the back is a long view of garden and fields beyond the reflecting pool and fountain.

Within the back garden are an abundant bulb planting and crape myrtle, Cherokee rose and camellias. The live oaks bear the whiskery fronds of Spanish moss not to be seen farther to the north along the Mississippi.

There is a huge terrace surrounded by redbud, dogwood, azalea, magnolias and poplars. The entire terrace is shaded by its central feature, a huge oak whose base is surrounded by a planting of aucuba and various varieties of holly. The fence around the terrace is a copy of an old Louisiana plantation fence. Painted to look like metal, it is actually of pegged wood. A small structure at the corner is the old necessary house which is to be converted to a more contemporary function. Beyond are open fields and cabins.

The house was built by William St. John Elliot, a relative of General John D'Evereux who fought at the side of Simon Bolivar. It is after the General that the house was named. Mr. Elliot left the house to his widow for her lifetime use but it was, at her death, to go to the Catholic Diocese to be used as a Catholic Boys' Orphanage. Mrs. Elliot, however, purchased the house from the Bishop who used the proceeds to establish the orphanage across town. It was called D'Evereux Hall so the word Hall was dropped from the house name and became, simply, D'Evereux.

D'Evereux's stateliness is matched only by its grace. Lovely ironwork and ceiling rosettes continue the elegance of design which is never florid or overstated at D'Evereux.

The portico looks out on camellias under the outstretched limbs of live oaks.

The orphanage lasted for 100 years. In 1967 it was torn down and the plaque memorializing the Elliots' generosity was given, along with the pre-Civil War school bell to the present owners of D'Evereux to be displayed here. It is likely that this was a plantation bell since its markings show it to have been cast in 1859. The base which displays the plaque was designed to repeat the design of the portico column bases. The bell housing is that which was used at the orphanage. Thus is recognition of the Elliots' philanthropy come home to rest.

The double drive was designed to dramatize the magnificent magnolia which stands near a wisteria-covered cedar fence. Beyond this fence and below is a great display of camellias which thrive under the outstretched curves of the live oak limbs.

One of the lovely features of the entire garden is a large dead cedar which is so completely shrouded by Cherokee rose that the effect is of a giant cascade of bloom. Since the cedar is practically impervious to rot it is apt to provide a quite permanent home for the rose . . . as the Buckleses are providing a home for beauty by maintaining D'Evereux as an open house.

The great terrace is circled by old Louisiana plantation fencing.

By day or by floodlit night D'Evereux stands beautiful for all passersby to enjoy.

Dr. and Mrs. R.H. Barnes
Natchez, Mississippi

Dr. Barnes is an extremely busy young surgeon with a passionate love of gardening as one of his principal interests and relaxants. Because the requirements of his profession limit his time for other pursuits, his garden must be easy to maintain. This is an old townhouse property with a small ground area. In the decade the Barnes' have lived here they have completely renovated the house and created the grounds. Now, they have acquired the adjoining property and leveled the structure, which had deteriorated beyond repair. On this lot an extension of the gardens will be built. The old brick from the demolition is stacked for future use in the new garden.

Between the sidewalk and the street is a row of crape myrtles whose graceful barkless forms have been pruned to emphasize their loveliness. The front porch of the house is faced with podocarpus just inside the wrought-iron fence whose gate leads to the bricked stone steps and to the small formal garden of brick walks and beds lined with low clipped English boxwood. The flower beds contain Southern daffodils, miniature yellow roses and coreopsis. A simple trellis bears Carolina jessamine. A unicorn does double duty as garden decoration and hobbyhorse for the neighborhood children.

Redbud and crape myrtle set off the introduction to the gardens behind the house. The curved walk is of stepping stones made from old ship ballast rock set in fine peastone gravel. A lawn area sets off the elevated azalea beds. Terracing throughout the entire garden was necessary to reduce the severity of runoff flow and drainage problems that exist because the property is at the base of a hill.

The private brick terrace and back gardens have as their center points a wisteria pergola and a sweet olive tree. Undulating brick retaining walls do multiple duty, providing soil and moisture retention, design and base and background for flowering shrubs,

yaupon, holly and variegated liriope. To complete the privacy of this area, a link fence covered with ivy was constructed. A triple trunk mulberry helps to relieve the severity of wall lines. At the end of the garden an espaliered loquat obscures the wall of the neighboring house. Potted plants, including oleander, complete the terrace design.

An elderly neighbor whose family had owned this property for five generations told Dr. Barnes that her childhood memories are of a garden not unlike the one he has made at the front of the house.

This is yet another of the townhouse gardens which demonstrate how successfully the designs and examples of the large gardens can be scaled to use in limited space and with limited time for maintenance.

Recognizing that the peculiar requirements caused by the terrain not only of the garden but by that of its neighbors, Dr. Barnes wisely sought professional consultative help in laying out a plan. J.D. Zachariah and Earl Hart Miller worked with Dr. Barnes to create this little jewel.

The force of the wisteria stem has twisted its host column.

Wisteria seems as natural to Natchez as the sun.

Hope Farm
Natchez, Miss.

Owned by the Millers for 41 years, Hope Farm was bought by them to save it from the demolition another prospective purchaser threatened because it had been allowed to deteriorate. Instead of demolition, the Millers gave the old house and grounds new life and a vitality like that of the vigorous young woman Mrs. Miller is in her mid-seventies.

The Millers are native Natchezians whose forebears settled here in the 1700s. Mrs. Miller has spearheaded the restoration, preservation and a promise of future for many of the great old homes of Natchez. She instigated the springtime Natchez Pilgrimage when the whole town plays festive host to visitors who flock here in great numbers to see the fabled beauty of this Mississippi garden paradise.

Hope Farm is not without its own ties to history, for Don Carlos de Grand Pre made it his home when he was the Spanish Governor of the territory. This is not a grand, imposing building of great, soaring columns and circling galleries. From the front it looks like a not-too-large one-story white farmhouse which might be seen anywhere. The front plantings on the banks and terrace before the house take visual precedence over the structure. The banks are heavily set in bulbs and ground cover. The terrace is two boxwood enclosures surrounding flower beds and walk arounds.

This is part of the original planting which remains as a guide to the character of very old Natchez garden design and content.

The more extensive gardens behind the house were created by Mrs. Miller over a period of fifteen years. She was in the position of learning while doing. Her natural taste and instincts directed her toward several basic goals for her garden: there must be a focal point; there must be an axis; and there must be vistas.

These basic intents were so well realized that a Garden Clubs of America President asked, while visiting here, "Who designed your garden for you?" She has achieved a totally individual expression of her love for place without locking herself into stultifying over-regard for tradition. She makes no pretense that her garden is a thing of horticultural perfection; instead, she loves even those things which a perfectionist might consider flaws. Her love is rightly given since these are the character givers which individualize this charming, rather wild garden. It demonstrates that good gardening, like good cooking, does not slavishly follow recipes written by someone else but uses them only as a base for creating something uniquely one's own.

At the back of the house comes the first awareness of its size. Because of the slope on which it was built, it is mostly two stories and with a long ell which helps to form a courtyard of the lawn space. There is an upper veranda from which may be seen the vista, the axis and the focal point. In the distance are two great pecan trees which are the focal point. The axis is provided by the stone basin in the courtyard. The gentle downward slope of the land provides the vista.

The pecans are covered with wisteria vines which give a lavender color to the trees behind which is a series of banksia roses so cultivated as to give the impression of yellow blooming trees.

The vistal view is dotted with great quantities of informally set bulbs which begin their blooming season in January along with the camellias near the house.

To the right side of the house is a large azalea garden set apart from a larger stretch of azaleas which form the garden to the left behind the house. In this garden is a nice note of artistic frugality—an antique chimney pot of good design and color is used as a garden pedestal.

This is a garden which brings the word pictures of William Faulkner to mind. Great, bladed fans hanging from veranda ceilings—a benevolent paternalism of divided oneness—a clinging to past glory—but above all, a quiet indomitability which says "my paint may be cracked but my heart beats strong."

This house originally stood on ten or twelve acres. Now it sits high above the streets around it, the sides of its hill having been cut away to level those streets. The house was built in two periods beginning in the 1700s. It faces, across the gully of pavement, the house called Choctaw. They are named after two of the Indian tribes which inhabited the region before the incursions of civilization drove them out.

This is one of the houses included in the Garden Tour of the Annual Natchez Pilgrimage that begins in the latter half of March. The Stanton Hall Mansion Restoration and the buildings behind it are a beehive of activity in which the work of arranging the details of the Pilgrimage is done. Stanton Hall was built on land which was part of the original holdings of Cherokee.

A stone bird basin is the axis around which the garden is set.

Hope Farm's gardens are rich with old-fashioned Southern country charm.

Cherokee
Natchez, Mississippi

Natchez was spared much of the destruction of the Civil War. Only one large house was said to have suffered from the vengeful pique of a Northern Officer who was not invited to a party. He had the house destroyed by declaring its center to be a battle line. Cherokee was especially fortunate since shells from the bombardment of the city fell on the grounds surrounding the house.

The entry at the base of the steps leading up to the house and grounds is beautified by a fine wrought-iron gate. The vertical sides of the grounds are retained by a lovely brick wall built by the present owners, Mr. and Mrs. Charles J. Byrne.

At the top of the stairs is the recessed front portico which forms a gracious entryway to the house. Beyond the front of the house is an azalea garden which also makes use of bulbs and pansies. It is the "Mauve Garden" whose blossom colors run from pink to violet. There is a small circular pool constructed over what was an old cistern. Background trees hide the view of the industrialized waterfront.

Continuing around the house is another garden which features salmon pink and white azaleas, tulips, white pansies and white dogwoods. In this section is an outdoor sitting terrace all shaded by a large Japanese Holly tree and Cunninghamia. Next is the upper terrace directly behind the house. It is "White Garden," featuring white petunias in the formal beds. In the center of the White Garden is displayed the top of an old stone plantation column. Cunningham yews, a species of Oriental conifers used in the Far East as plantings around temples, form the screening background on two sides of the upper terrace. Between the house and the garden is a brick-paved terrace.

Along the east side of the house overlooking the street below is a planting of gardenias and camellias which thrive in Natchez. There is no feeling here of front or back.

There are instead, a series of gardens in a ring around the house.

Although, or perhaps because, Cherokee is located in an area of Natchez which contains warehouses and other commercial structures, its presence is a constant reminder of the necessity for Natchez and other waterfront cities to reclaim the non-commercial enjoyment and beauty of natural waterfronts. If this comes to be, Cherokee will be a focal point of beauty within beauty. As it is, Cherokee stands as an elevated fortress of beauty holding urban blight at bay.

The lower terrace garden features salmon pink azaleas.

Recessed portico entry to Cherokee.

Beauvoir
Biloxi, Mississippi

The Gulf Coast is a heartrending sight. The hurricane of August, 1969, slashed the shoreline buildings and trees to shreds. Between the force of the wind and the smashing seawater driving inland, there was little that was spared the storm's devastation. Fortunately, Beauvoir's buildings were among those that came through almost unscathed.

There are three gardens to be written about at Beauvoir; the garden that is; the garden that was before the hurricane; and the garden that was planned as the Confederate Memorial Gardens. The last, despite elaborate preparations and a complete projected financial plan proposed in 1953, never materialized, but the plans are worthy of delineation as a dream which remained just a dream.

The garden that was before the storm was the garden that Jefferson Davis enjoyed in the last twelve years of his life. He enjoyed being a flower gardener and dirt farmer. Almost daily he walked, rowed or rode on these grounds and waters. He loved to sit by the little spring with its natural surroundings. There were all the semitropical plants native to the area, plus azaleas, camellias, loquats and Mrs. Davis' beloved rose garden. All of this was maintained as a natural garden without formal design as befitted the quiet dignity of the man who lived and worked here.

The garden that was proposed as a shrine to the Confederacy and its President was conceived to honor the participation of the eleven states which seceded from the Union and fought on the Southern side in the Civil War.

It would have been developed around Beauvoir House, with eleven state memorials and a court of flags with extensive plantings to provide masses of bloom utilizing the various state flowers. Such floral displays would have been an echo of the words Jefferson Davis wrote for the title page of his two-volume work *Rise and Fall of the Confederate Government:*

"To the women of the Confederacy whose pious ministrations to our wounded soldiers soothed the last hours of those who died far from the objects of their tenderest love; whose domestic labors contributed much to supply the wants of our defenders in the field; whose zealous faith in our cause shone a shining star undimmed by the darkest clouds of war; whose fortitude sustained under all the privations to which they were subjected; whose floral tribute annually expresses their enduring love and reverence for our sacred dead; and whose patriotism will teach their children to emulate the deeds of our revolutionary sires; these pages are dedicated by their countryman."

The garden that exists is the remainder left by the savagery of the tropical storm. The work of cleaning up and replacing lost plantings continues but little can be done to hurry the desalinization of the soil which lay under four feet of seawater. In time the old garden will be reborn to make again a lovely place by the sea where people come to pay homage to the hero of their defeat.

This building was constructed in about 1737 on a French land grant when the Gulf Coast was under French control. No record remains of the size of the original grant but in 1820 the holdings consisted of 485.34 acres.

The house is of solid brick construction with heart pine beams, sills and woodwork. The verticals are wooden pegged columns of cypress. The two ironbracing beams that run through the attic show on the exterior in the form of an "S."

The roofing and porch flooring are of slate brought from France as ship ballast. The porch flooring pieces are four-inch thick, twenty-inch squares. Such construction enabled the house to withstand the hurricane which destroyed many of its neighbors.

Though standing close to the sea, Beauvoir has been spared serious damage.

A rarity in Gulf Coast buildings is the brick walled and floored cellar so dry that it was once used for the storage of books. Now it is the wine cellar for the outstanding restaurant which the building houses. The spacious garden court is enclosed by a high brick wall once adorned with scuppernong grapevines. The focal point of the garden is the magnificent live oak whose age has been variously placed at from 500 to 2000 years. Since the salt air is said to slow the development of live oaks, it is entirely possible that this was a mature giant when Columbus discovered the New World.

The gardens, like the building, are meticulously maintained and repair work and replanting made necessary by storm damage continues. Much of the garden soil has been completely replaced and, when the work is done, all the soil will have been brought in to provide fertile homes for the plantings whose beds were made inhospitable by the saline waters which covered them in 1969. The gardener works assiduously to complete this task of reclamation.

The garden court is a semiformal garden. There is a definite plan and pattern established by the brick walks and brick-edged bedding areas, but there is no use of boxwood or other hedging growth to reduce the airy openness which gives the garden its spaciousness.

Young "sago palm" provides a deep green accent close to the ground. Bird of paradise blooms in unusual decorative pots. Bishop's cap gives a bright red accent with its bloom and berry. Hibiscus, palm and bamboo lend a lush, tropical air to the outdoor dining patio while the ferns provide a note of forest cool near ground level. Inside these walls it is hard to remember that only a few feet away stand the shattered remnants of storm-torn old buildings less fortunate than the French House.

This gate is the monument to Jefferson Davis, President of the Confederacy.

Old French House Restaurant Garden

Biloxi, Mississippi

Across Water Street is the old Spanish House, built in 1780, before the Louisiana Purchase. It is a distinctive structure which shows, in its proximity to the Old French House, the Architectural differences between these two cultures and periods of Biloxi history. This garden, too, is being restored to its characteristically simple Spanish form.

The internationality of this part of Biloxi is broadened by the owner and operator of the French House Restaurant which is just as well known in Biloxi as Mary Mahoney's.

This woman, married to an Irishman, is of Yugoslavian ancestry. The chef and maître d' is Italian and most of the employees are native Biloxi blacks. Mary Mahoney née Cvitanovich feels that she operates her own little United Nations beneath "the Patriarch," as the great live oak is known. This atmosphere is heightened by the paintings displayed and painted directly on the walls by artists of the Mississippi Coast Art Association who were invited by Mrs. Mahoney to paint whatever they pleased.

Fountain cherub livens a corner of the garden.

It has been necessary to replace most of the salt-water soaked soil to keep the garden fertile.

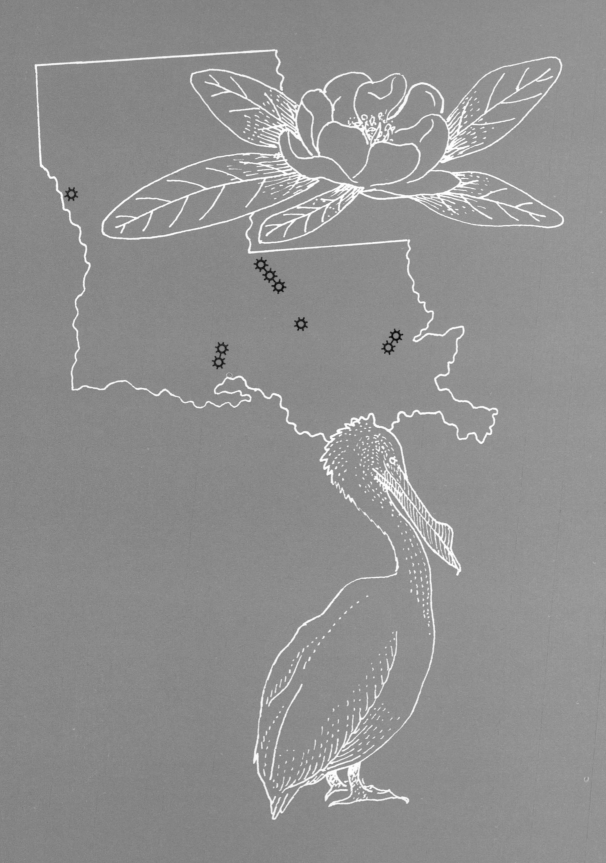

LOUISIANA

Afton Villa
Feliciana Parish, St. Francisville, La.

Afton Villa was so named because of the placid waters which flow nearby. Part of a Spanish land grant, it was the first settlement in "West Florida," as this territory was then called by the Spanish. It is in this area that the first evidence of bayou country is seen, if you are coming from the north.

The house, or more correctly, the two houses in one which stood here until a few years ago were built over a period of many years. First, there was a modest cottage that served until the 1840s when it was enclosed by the great, 40-room mansion that was built around it. This large structure was created in a style foreign to the antebellum Greek Revival style that was generally used during that period. It was a house built for a new bride. It is said that the honeymooning couple saw, in France, a Chateau in Tours which they wanted to duplicate, and that they brought from France the architect and builder of the chateau. Pictures of the house indicate that the results were something different from most French chateaux. It was a highly ornamented building more reminiscent of Victorian styling with oriental overtones.

The entry to the property is made down a very long, winding oak allée at whose bases are plantings of alternating azaleas and bridal wreath. The silver gray, sunlit moss draped from the trees lends a romantically ominous note to the drive—a note which comes to fullness when the drive end is reached and no house is to be seen.

Afton Villa burned to the ground a few years ago when the mistress of the house neglected the kitchen stove when she went to attend her sick husband. The foundation remains are rubble-strewn and weed-grown now with only the outline to tell of the size of the old house.

It is a strange sight to look at the ruins and then look to the left only a few feet away and see a lovely formal double garden with a wide separating lane and fountained circle.

One half of this double garden is a wonderfully intricate boxwood maze in which roses are the principal planting. The other half displays in its boxwood enclosed bedding areas camellias and azaleas, one of which is the famed Afton azalea.

Past these formal beds is a broad sweep of descending lawn and steps in a series of seven terraces which, with the trees and growth beyond, look like the old England of the sweet Afton.

Enclosed by a high hedge is an island in this sea of lawn. It is the old family burying ground whose many stones indicate that there must have been some sort of virulent epidemic in the years of 1845 and 1846. People of the area say that it must have been yellow fever. Whatever it was must have decimated the residents of Afton Villa.

Seven terraces comprise the long, sloping stretch of lawn from garden to bayou woods.

There is, beyond the edge of great lawn, a second oak allée leading to what had been the Bayou Sara landing for the plantation. Coincidentally, or perhaps through design, it bears the same name as the Barrow bride for whom the Villa was built.

The broad sweep of Afton's lawns merges and blends gently into the surrounding lushness of thick growth characteristic of a moist, semitropical country. The gentleness of the terrace drops gives the impression that they were natural, but they were man-made to give more interest to the open stretch of greensward.

Afton's present owner feels that if the time should come when he would build a new residence on the property its style should be in complete harmony with the history and character of the surroundings. It would not incorporate any of the form of the burned-out predecessor structure. It would probably be a combination of the best features of English, Spanish and Western American architecture blended into one simple form. This is a sound desire since each of these cultures has contributed to the history of Afton Villa.

In the meantime, the gardens and outbuildings will be maintained and not allowed to suffer the neglect that too often befalls such a property after the house has been destroyed.

The atmosphere and effect of Afton are not dissimilar to what is felt when drifting lazily on a slow flowing stream. It divorces one from the cares of the commercial, competitive world and totally saturates the being with a placid disassociation with strife.

A quartered circle separates the double gardens.
This was the axial view from the steps of the house.

One half of the formal gardens is the maze rose garden.

Rosedown Plantation and Gardens
St. Francisville, Louisiana

Along the great river road which runs from Natchez to New Orleans are many of the fine, old, once-prosperous plantations that enriched Southern history and Southern economy. Some have deteriorated, some have burned, some have been restored to their original beauty. One of the fortunate ones is Rosedown which had, and has, unusually fine and extensive gardens on three sides of the house. It was all built by Daniel Turnbull whose wealth and aristocratic tastes combined to provide an elegance unusual even to this opulent place and time. He and his wife, Martha, toured Europe collecting fine furnishings and the statuary which still lines the long oak avenue.

After the Civil War, Martha Turnbull joined the genteel new Southern poor in a style of life to which none of them was accustomed. Mrs. Turnbull, a remarkable horticulturist for her day, was possessed of a strong character which asserted itself and sustained her over the long, difficult years of her poverty till she died at 87 in 1896.

She kept a diary which records sixty years of her gardening at Rosedown. This diary was the guide for the ten years of work which restored the gardens. To save her gardens from the deterioration they were suffering as weeds and wild growth took over, she hired, however she could, former slaves to do the necessary chores. "Julia one week at 40 cents. . . . Penny and Lancaster 2 days each, $1.60. . . . Penny cleaning front yard, gave her 2 lbs. coffee, 2 lbs. sugar . . . Pint Molasses . . . Ben hawled all leaves from The Avenue . . . Kitty and children cleaned up with Clabber paying." The above is one of the entries in the diary. Then, as times worsened, there was this entry; "August 23rd . . . cleaned up my yard entirely by my own hands and now hawling manure and trash from Eliza's side."

This was a token of what was to continue for almost a century of struggle. After Martha Turnbull's death the house and land were inherited by her daughter who had married the son of the same Eliza Pirrie whose tutorial needs had brought John James Audubon to nearby Oakley. Four spinster granddaughters of Martha were next to inherit the burdensome task of preserving as best they could with their own hands what remained of Rosedown's gardens. They succeeded in maintaining enough of the twenty-eight and a half acres sufficiently well to inspire a Houston couple, Milton and Catherine Fondren Underwood, to buy Rosedown and achieve full restoration of house and grounds.

Mrs. Underwood called in Ralph Ellis Gunn, landscape architect of Houston. He assured her that the gardens could be saved and that the grounds contained one of the most unusual horticultural collections in America. Thorough research of the papers stored at Rosedown and study of the diary indicated that the gardens had not, as legend had it, been designed by a Parisian landscape architect, but by Martha Turnbull herself.

Another invaluable aid to the restorers was a WPA architect's survey of Rosedown made in the 1930s by Richard Koch. By this survey they were to locate a number of paths which had been overgrown, the potting shed, greenhouse, and conservatory, and were able to identify a brick wall as the remains of the greenhouse.

Today, this elegant mansion and its magnificent grounds represent a complete museum of the Old South and its way of life.

The rose gardens are a preserve where the oldest varieties, so long neglected in favor of contemporary hybrids, are given the places of honor they deserve as the representatives of antiquity in horticulture. The stunning rose hedges are of burr roses, known as chinquapin roses in the South. Its foliage is

The arch of the long oak allée frames the first view of Rosedown.

like the locust, unlike the leaves of any other rose. The two-toned flat pink roses emerge from little bristly buds that resemble a chinquapin burr. Bristles appear even on the seed pods. The burr rose has gray-green mottled bark which it sheds as the sycamore tree sheds its bark. The flowers, deep pink at the center with outer petals of pale pink, bloom heavily in the spring, intermittently in the summer, and generously in the fall.

Neat beds bordered by boxwood hedges house a wide variety of other ancient roses, some of which are seldom out of bloom. There is a China rose sometimes called Shipwreck rose because of the legend which says that it reached these shores from a ship that was wrecked.

Set in the garden is a small building which was the plantation doctor's office and home. It contains all the equipment to be found in a physician's office of those days, plus dental care equipment since the doctor did double duty as dentist and medical practitioner. It has long been said in the South that the slaves received better medical care than did the blacks after emancipation. Here is evidence that this was probably true.

However, the reason for this care should not be overlooked. It was to the owner's interest that people who were considered valuable chattel property be maintained in good health and working condition. As a result, the plantation doctor was one of the most important members of its community.

This part of Louisiana was aptly named by the Spanish rulers, Feliciana, which means "happy land." It has had its unhappy times in recent history, but today, thanks to its people, it has begun to smile again. This eastern side of the lower Mississippi is as different in its cultural aspects from the western, or alluvial side as are its topographical characteristics. The eastern side reflects the English heritage of the settlers and the western side reflects the French.

Nowhere, on either side of the great river, is to be found any place more completely reflective of the luxury and grandeur of plantation living than at Rosedown. And nowhere is there stronger evidence of the valiant character and strength of "frail" womanhood's struggle to keep beauty alive in a troubled land.

Entrance to the Rose Gardens is lined with rose hedges.

Little boy and dolphin fountain of Carrera marble is only one of a large collection of statuary at Rosedown.

Plantation doctor's office is a tiny treasure in itself.

Oakley
Feliciana Parish, La.

Because it was here that the great naturalist, John James Audubon, did much of his important work of drawing the birds and flowers which abounded in Feliciana Parish, it is widely known as "Audubon's Happy Land."

Oakley House was begun in 1799 by Ruffin Gray of Natchez who died before the house was complete. His widow married a Scotsman, James Pirrie, to whom she bore a daughter, Eliza. It was Eliza's need for a tutor that brought Audubon to Oakley in 1821. He was in difficult financial straits since his work on the monumental *Birds of America* was not immediately revenue-productive. He needed to maintain himself, his thirteen year old pupil-assistant, John Mason, and his work. He arranged with the Pirries to come to Oakley, and spent half his time as a tutor, teaching Eliza drawing, music and dance. The other half of the working day he was to be free to roam the woods to study and work on his paintings. This employment earned for Audubon sixty dollars a month, room and board for himself and young Mason and the opportunity to study firsthand the area rich in avian life. Of his arrival at Bayou Sara and Oakley, he wrote: "The aspect of the country was entirely new to me and distracted my mind from those objects which are the occupation of my life. The rich magnolias covered with fragrant blossoms, the holly, the beech, the tall yellow poplar, the hilly ground and even the red clay, all excited my admiration. Such an entire change in the face of nature in so short a time seems almost supernatural; and surrounded once more by numberless warblers and thrushes, I enjoyed the scene. The five miles we walked appeared short, and we arrived and met Mr. Pirrie at his house . . . we were received kindly."

But Audubon's happy relationship with the land proved more enduring than with his employers and after a four-month stay he returned to New Orleans. While at Oakley, in this brief time, Audubon painted thirty-two of the bird pictures which are among his important early works. Audubon's wife and son lived on in West Feliciana for seven years during which time she worked as a teacher.

After accumulating two thousand dollars from his own tutorial activities Audubon rejoined his family here and, by pooling their savings, Audubon was enabled to continue his ornithological work and travel to England where his work was reproduced through the medium of steel engravings.

Peahens stroll the walks of the gardens along with human visitors.

Oakley House has its own architectural importance. Preceding the classic revival employed in so many great plantation houses, it possesses a less imposing but nonetheless effective simple, unornamented beauty all its own. The tall, jalousied galleries provide cool ventilation for the main living rooms of the interior.

At one side of the house is a formal garden in the English manner—the work of the ladies of the Garden Study Club of New Orleans. The white picket fence makes this garden seem an extension of the house from whose upper floors it may be viewed to great advantage. It is called the Rose Garden but its pink camellias serve to bring color when the roses are dormant.

The walks to the house are lined with Ardisia whose brilliant red berries glow like live coals against the green foliage. The Rose Garden and the approach to the house are the only cultivated parts of the 100-acre Audubon Memorial State Park now owned by the State of Louisiana. The rest is being preserved in its natural state as Audubon knew it. The nature trails are rich in the floral and avian life which provided the great naturalist with so much inspiration and material for study. What he captured on paper is free to live at Oakley. It is a nature which repays affection with a soft embrace. All it asks is that it be allowed to bring life and joy of life.

White picket fence and pink brick paving accent the small garden's formality.

The jalousies of Oakley's galleries are an unusual note along the Mississippi.

Belle Helene (Ashland)
Ascension Parish, Geismar, Louisiana

Built in 1837 to 1841 and called Ashland by Duncan Farrar Kenner, Belle Helene is a tatterdemalion relic of a colorful past in the area which produced most of America's antebellum millionaires. Now, Belle Helene is threatened with engulfment and strangulation by the chemical plants and their pipelines which surround it with structures and with effluents spewed into the air.

Weed-grown and unkempt, the beauty of Belle Helene still comes through the atmosphere of long neglect which pervades house and grounds.

Duncan Kenner was one of the largest slave owners of the South. During "the War" in 1864 he served as Confederate Minister to France and England.

The house was built for his bride who was born and was married on the 28th day of the month. To commemorate this number the house was designed with twenty-eight great columns. In planting the grounds twenty-eight live oaks were set in as part of the horseshoe pattern of trees which enclose the house. At the foot of this unique allée the trees are set in the shape of a horse's hoof. Thus did Kenner pay tribute to his two great loves, his bride and the breeding, raising and racing of horses on his own track.

The plantation's fortune was based on sugarcane. Tremendous sugarcane kettles "lie" in haphazard array around the old mansion along with a huge rice stone and an upside-down corn grinder.

The garden's fountain pool is cracked and empty of water but the kettles serve as oversize birdbaths for the large flocks which make this place their winter home.

Restoration work is being done by Mr. William Hayward, Sr., husband of the present owner, with money being earned on his own sugarcane plantation. The patches of dirt which serve as floor where wood has been removed, the cracked and falling plaster of walls and ceilings, the vandalized,

Twenty-eight great columns go around the house to commemorate the birth and wedding date of the bride for whom it was built.

The fountain pool is cracked and empty but Louisiana sugar kettles lying in disarray on the ground catch rainwater and serve the birds which abound at Belle Helene.

mantelless fireplaces of the first floor give testimony to the ravages of time and unwanted attention. None of this is to be seen on the second floor whose rooms have been receiled and plastered as the first steps toward restoration.

The brick paving on the first floor gallery was restored by the movie producers who worked here in 1970 making a Civil War Saga for whose scenes a down-at-the-heels Southern mansion was necessary. This was not the first time that Belle Helene played hostess to the cinematic world. In 1957, the late Clark Gable acted before cameras set in and around the house and gazebo.

The gates and pillars which stand at the entry to the allée were built and left to stand by the movie makers of 1970.

Belle Helene's skin is wrinkled and blemished with the tarnish of neglect, her green leaf and floral dress is tattered and stained, but her bones are strong. As implacably as the wisteria vine, she clings with gnarled and desiccated hands to a beauty too great to be totally destroyed by inattention. As though buoyed in spirit by the fragrance of sweet olive and rose she patiently waits in her imperishable splendor to be brought again to full flower by the gallant old gentleman of ninety-two who is married to the woman after whom the house was renamed by her grandfather, John Reuss, who bought Ashland from the Kenners in the 1870s.

From sugarcane, antebellum glory to years of neglect to aged movie star being rejuvenated by earnings from sugarcane—this is the romantic story of a true Southern Belle, Belle Hélene née Ashland.

Even in its present, unrestored condition, Belle Helene's beauty and purity of line stand noble against the sky.

Ursuline Convent
Chartres St., New Orleans

Across the street from the old Royal Botanical Gardens which no longer exist is the Convent Garden whose present plantings are a replica of the Royal Botanical which ceased to be in the 1760s.

A military hospital which was adjacent to the Botanical Gardens was built in 1722 after a hurricane. It soon proved inadequate to the needs of a fever-ridden city. The Convent was built between 1727 and 1734. Attached to it was a new, larger hospital built in 1733. It was administered by the Ursuline nuns who were sent to New Orleans for the express purpose of tending the sick. The nuns also established a girls' school which is still operating.

With Spanish acquisition of New Orleans the new rulers took over the hospital and the nuns devoted all of their time and attention to the school. In 1824 the nuns moved to a new convent when they gave the old building to the Bishop to be his residence. In 1828, the old convent, while still serving to house the Bishop also provided a meeting place for several sessions of the state legislature. It remained the Bishop's residence until 1899. The building then served as a seminary and as the archdiocesan offices until 1919 when the adjacent church, St. Mary's Italian was turned over to the Oblate Fathers who have since used the convent as a rectory in which they perform community work, part of which is the counseling of the many young people who frequent and live in the French Quarter.

Originally the garden was on the opposite, or river, side of the building. It can safely be conjectured that the garden contained herbs as well as vines, fruit trees and flowers.

When the Bishop took over the premises he elaborated the rear garden which became, with the creation of Chartres Street, the front. It was he who built the gate house which still stands. Then, in 1941, a garden based on the plans of the old French Royal Botanical Garden, was laid out by Edward Woolbright. This is the garden which exists today in the French Quarter with its world famous Bohemian atmosphere likened by many to the Left Bank in Paris.

The present planting in a six-area parterre was the work of the Patio Planters, the Garden Club of the Vieux Carré. Mrs. Charles Colby was the guiding and inspirational force who raised the money for the project and obtained the cooperation of the city with the proviso that the garden be open to the public. The city still maintains the gardens. The pleasure of viewing the garden is enhanced by the sound of organ music emanating from the adjacent church.

Six parterres make up the garden which is a replica of the old Royal Botanical Gardens.

The Ursuline Convent and its garden possess a heritage of French, Spanish and American culture so evident in this setting of the Vieux Carré. It is a national historic landmark, having been granted this distinction with the institution of that program though the formal presentation of the plaque was made in 1968.

The quiet of this historic corner of the French Quarter is in sharp contrast to the Bohemian business and hip talk of the surroundings which reflect the most contemporary dissidence.

Across Chartres street from the Ursuline Convent on land which the Ursulines sold in 1824 a man named Carpentier built this house. The years 1866-1868 were the time when the house was the residence of the great Confederate General P. G. T. Beauregard.

This property has two gardens, one on the corner, and one behind the house is a small, private patio garden. The large, corner garden was recently laid out in its original plan by architect Samuel Wilson, Jr.

This residence having been the home of Frances Parkinson Keyes is now owned by the Keyes Foundation. The garden is presently being replanted with growth characteristic of the gardens of its antebellum days. This work is being done by the ladies of the Garden Study Clubs of New Orleans, the same group which did the garden at Oakley.

The fountain in the patio garden was found and shipped to New Orleans from a Vermont village by Mrs. Keyes. The office in which she wrote opens directly onto the patio. Originally, the four corners contained crape myrtle but one of these was ousted by a volunteer oak which, in 20 years has attained massive size and shades the entire garden. This is the only old New Orleans house which had and has a side and back garden.

Garden areas such as this which can be seen through the wrought-iron gates on Chartres and Ursulines Streets are a welcome break in the pastel phalanxes of buildings standing shoulder to shoulder to form the solid borders of the Vieux Carré streets.

Some of the house's old history is being re-enacted in early 1971 as it gives an authentic setting for a period-adventure drama of the 1830s being filmed within its walls. The central and title character of the piece is one of the quadroon mistresses who were a part of the old New Orleans scene in the days when sumptuous mansions were built for brides and elegant town quarters were provided for mistresses of darker hue.

The Carpentier-Beauregard property was once part of the garden of the Ursulines.

Bird songs and organ music add to the visual beauty of the garden in the Old French Quarter.

Longue Vue Gardens
New Orleans, Louisiana

To the great loss of many potential visitors, the existence of this exquisite garden is relatively unknown. The concept, execution and maintenance are such that this unfortunate anonymity is sure to be soon replaced by well-deserved fame.

Longue Vue took its name from an old estate on the Hudson River where Longue Vue's founder, Mrs. Edith Stern, became engaged to her husband, the late Edgar B. Stern. Longue Vue was originally designed by the late Ellen Shipman. Loggia and fountains were added in 1952. With Mrs. Stern, William Platt redesigned the Spanish Garden following a visit to Granada in 1966. Inspired by the Generalife Garden at Granada, the Spanish is the largest of the sequence of gardens which make up Longue Vue. As magnificent and important as it is in size and beauty, the Spanish Garden in no way diminishes the loveliness or significance of the more intimate gardens which complete the chain. The first of these, designed by Mrs. Stern, is the Yellow Garden where blooms of that color are in evidence all year around a small fountain pool. The contemporary fountain sculpture, designed by Robert Engman, is so right for its location that its contemporary quality weds tradition without any trace of anachronism. The flow of water falling from the fountain causes an eye catching swirl which constantly eddies in the pool.

Close to the main house is the Portico Garden whose main feature is the formal parterre of boxwood-bordered beds containing tree roses, camellias, fragrant sweet olives and podocarpus. Outer borders are solid plantings of floribunda rose "Summer Snow." It is in the character of a multilevel English clipped garden which guides the eye to its larger neighbor. Around the house to the left, past extensive· terrace plantings of roses and a sweep of broad lawn is the small Pan Garden on one wall of which is a plaque in memory of its designer, Ellen Shipman. Another wall features a statue of Pan sculpted by the English artist, Josephine Knoblock. In addition to the camellias, roses, azaleas, magnolias and podocarpus, this garden is planted with bulbs, caladium, chrysanthemum and cyclamen. From the Pan Garden is a long view across garden lawn and adjacent golf course fairways. This great open sweep emphasizes the gentle intimacy of the shaded garden.

To the left, across the lawn, is the parking area which exemplifies the philosophy of devotion to total beauty which is evident all through Longue Vue. This parking court is paved with dual-toned concrete blocks of dark gray and white whose design and finish could grace a Palace floor. There are not many places in the world so complete in the loveliness of every detail that even the parking surface is a thing of beauty. Like the Yellow Garden, it was designed by Mrs. Stern.

Back at the Portico Garden, sweeping to the south, is the majestic stretch of the Spanish Garden. This view affords an all-encompassing sight of fountains, lawn, reflecting pool, colonnaded loggia, walls, planter boxes and stone walkways.

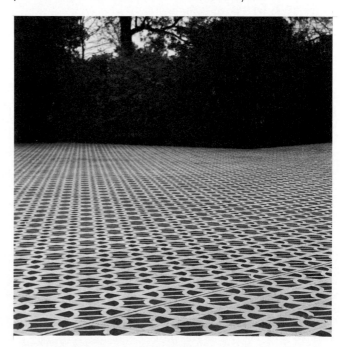

Even the Parking Court at Longue Vue is a design masterpiece.

The loggia pool alternates between functioning as a reflecting pool and a recipient of the arches of water which form a liquid double pleached allée which sparkles and dances like a jewelled ballerina in the sunlight.

The walkways are paved with stone from Spain, France and Georgia. Pebbles from Mexico, set on end, provide design frameworks for the walkways. Like so many beautiful things, this arrangement is also utilitarian since it provides sure footing in places kept moist by the mist blown from the cascade built into the walls and from the many fountains. Most of these are the work of the present landscape architect, William Platt. The delightful dolphin fountain of marble was rendered in Seville, Spain.

Water, greensward and evergreen growth are the dress of a Spanish garden. Floral plants are used only as accent jewels. Here, this is accomplished with planter boxes that flank the walkways.

Behind the loggia is the narrow Canal Garden which leads to the gate of the Walled Garden. Octagonal in shape, the Walled Garden develops around its central focus, a great sunken Louisiana sugar kettle. It is a pool fed from a wall fountain by way of the narrow, brick canal of the preceding garden. Rising in steps from the pool are plantings of iris, delphinium and chrysanthemum all to be viewed as from the top of an amphitheater. Borders around this center area are planted with Fielders' and Kings' white azaleas.

Beyond the other gate of the Walled Garden is the Wild Garden, all of native plant material through which run three nature trails that converge at the rock garden spring and circle the pool floored with Mississippi sandstone. The still waters of the pool reflect the growth, the rocks and, at the far end, the lovely pigeonnaire set in the woods.

The nursery area glows with a year round display of blossom in the gentle climate of New Orleans which knows no cessation of bloom and rich verdure.

The entrance court, the grand allée and the forecourt of the house are held to a dramatic simplicity as a quiet introduction to the beauty to be met beyond the wall.

Though this is a series of very individual gardens, there is a feeling of continuity which flows like the water from one area to the next. It is a feeling as constant as the quality and taste which distinguish Longue Vue. Splashy overuse of flamboyant flowers is avoided here where emphasis is on variety of color, subdued color, and advantageous display of color which may be enjoyed around the calendar. Through much of the South it is said during the winter, "Oh! This is such a bad time to see the gardens." This cannot be said at Longue Vue where any time is a good time to see and enjoy.

As a result of Mrs. Stern's philanthropy Longue Vue is now owned and operated as a civic and educational enterprise by Longue Vue Foundation.

The dolphin fountain was created for Longue Vue in Seville, Spain.

The nature garden is thick with lush sub tropical growth.

The avenue and forecourt of the house are deliberately understated as a quiet introduction to the gardens beyond.

Rip Van Winkle Gardens
Jefferson Island, Louisiana

West of New Orleans lies the "Cajun" country, Acadiana, where the descendants of transplanted French Canadians carry on their traditions of language, life-style, and cuisine.

Near New Iberia which is in the heart of Acadiana are several "islands" that are not islands in the sense of land surrounded by water. These are hills surrounded by flat marshlands. The hills are soil-covered domes of rock salt which, aeons ago, were pushed up from the mother bed five to eight miles below the surface of the coastal flats. Evident to the eye are only the small tips of these gigantic cones which are actually great underground rock salt mountains.

One of these islands is named for Joseph Jefferson, the great American actor of the last century. Its twenty acres of gardens memorialize the character he brought to life in the Washington Irving play, *Rip Van Winkle*.

At the height of a remarkable career Jefferson bought what was then known as Orange Island to establish a retreat from the pressures of a hectic life. He designed the home which still stands in the ornate "Steamboat Gothic" fashion of its time of building. It was constructed of cypress cut on the estate. Much of the carving of beams and interior framing is in the Moorish designs Jefferson had seen when he visited Irving at Granada while the author was Ambassador to Spain.

If Jefferson was the good actor in the island's history, the pirate Jean Lafitte might be said to be its "bad actor." Lafitte's brother-in-law owned the place which provided a haven and hiding place for the outlaw. Old tales that Lafitte buried booty here were somewhat substantiated in 1923 when a voodoo doctor named Daynite dug up three pots of old Spanish, Mexican, French, and American coins. The owner of the property bought the treasure from Daynite, though the witch doctor was an employee.

Local superstition has it that Lafitte's treasure must only be sought at night in the dark of the moon since moonlight striking the metal would drive the find deeper and deeper into the ground. If this were to happen it would only reveal the treasure which is certainly here: The diamonds that men use in their food and call salt; the black gold that provides fuel; and the yellow gold called sulphur.

In 1917, the late J. Lyle Bayless, Sr. bought Jefferson Island as a second home and began to develop the gardens near the house. His son and namesake, the present owner, was introduced at an early age to the joys of horticulture and after World War II began to spend more and more of his time and efforts in the expansion of the gardens. In 1957, he sold the salt mine and made the gardens his life work.

The private patio of the house has the isolation of a small tropical island.

Stone brought from faraway converted a glen into this lovely rock garden.

Hodges, Louisiana

Rosedown, Louisiana

Rip Van Winkle, Louisiana

Rosedown, Louisiana

D'Evereux, Mississippi

Cherokee, Mississippi

Rip Van Winkle, Louisiana

Hodges, Louisiana

Within the garden gates the open flatness of the surrounding countryside is immediately forgotten as the mystical magic of lush, moss-draped growth works its shadowy charm and erases thoughts of the world outside.

The first outlook is barely seen as the path leads into the seclusion of a bamboo- and camellia-enclosed iris garden whose pool may be traversed by means of large, circular stepping stones. A bamboo shelter stands invitingly by the walkway of old Scandinavian millstones. Through the bamboo thicket the Spanish well may be seen, its bottom glistening with coins tossed in by wish-makers.

The wrought-iron overstructure of the well is like a crown at the head of the Spanish-Moorish "Alhambra" garden which drops down a series of terraces, each with its own fountain, culminating in a graceful crescent pool and fountain at the lowest level.

At the left and below is another enclosed dell whose waters tumbling through and over the rocks of this garden lend a special pastoral quality, irresistible in its power to hold. The stone seats are like magnets pulling humans to quiet moments of restful appreciation of the rich contrast of rock texture and floral color on breeze wafted foliage.

A walk through thick, tropical growth leads to Lafitte's lawn at the edge of which are the unusual twin live oaks named for the pirate because the treasure was uncovered beneath them.

The Glen, shadowy and fern-cool, leads to the old fashioned Camellia Garden with its large specimens of *camellia japonica*.

The Crape Myrtle Allée is richly planted with a wide variety of spring and summer bloom which frames the view of the Great Lawn across which are the first view of the Jefferson house and the row of live oaks, the largest of which is named for the man who was twice President, Grover Cleveland. He came here often and took his afternoon siestas in the shade of this tree.

The Magnolia Walk, the herbaceous borders, and the grounds around the house are preludes to the winding path through the Little Boy Garden and the Wildflower Refuge. This path, planted with cycads, azaleas, hydrangeas, agapanthus, taro, mahonia, arresia, acacia, oleander, gardenia, photinia, banana, and leatherleaf fern opens on the Cascade topped by the Moon Window Seat. The original design of the Cascade included thirteen steps, thirteen pools, and thirteen waterfalls. Three times thirteen, however, held dire foreboding in local voodoo superstition so one pool, one step, and one waterfall were removed.

The Lafitte Twin Oaks named for the pirate, Jean Lafitte.

209

The fountain at the Moon Window Seat is a huge sugar kettle bordered by white Kurume azaleas, white oriental wisteria, and podocarpus.

Down the slope toward the lagoon is a lovely little Japanese Garden with an overlook patio which gives a fine view of Lafitte's Lagoon and Lake Peigneur.

At the water's edge is the landing where visitors may arrive by the sternwheel paddle boat, "Cajun Belle." She uses the same waterways which permitted Lafitte's shallow draft boats to come here where the deep draft ships of his pursuers could not follow.

Up the hill is the broad lawn of Peigneur Park bordered by tulips and azaleas which range in color from white to palest pink to fuchsia to crimson red. The white petunias and lemon yellow tulips complete the color palette of the Park.

At the top of the hill is a long channel of green at the end of which is the Chalice, an elevated sugar cauldron used as an aerial planter. It has become the symbol of Rip Van Winkle Gardens.

On March 14, 1971, the Chalice was the site for a wedding which joined two beautiful young people in a ceremony as symbolic of the oneness of men and the unity between man and nature as it was symbolic of the joining of a young man and a young woman. They chose this place because it exemplifies their value priorities.

On the broad lawn, flying kites, strolling through bamboo thickets, or sitting on the stones of the rock garden, the newlyweds and their friends were identifying with the universality of all things good. As they aptly put it, "the vibrations are all fine in this place."

The Alhambra Garden is only one of a series of garden areas at Rip Van Winkle.

Joe Jefferson home at Rip Van Winkle Gardens.

Jungle Gardens
Avery Island, Louisiana

As its name implies, Jungle Gardens is a rich, tropical growth which gives a natural home to alligators, egrets and other avifauna.

This is not a carefully trimmed and sculpted creation. It is a great collection of temperate, subtropical, and tropical plants from the whole world, planted and allowed to grow in natural groupings and settings that cover more than two hundred and fifty acres of the salt dome hill called Avery Island.

Just inside the gates huge flocks of herons and snowy egrets swoop and soar over water and come to rest in trees and on the specially built nesting places above the cruising guardians of the pond and swamp, the alligators.

Groves of timber bamboo and edible bamboo sweep up the hill as a foreground to a massive display of azaleas. Palms and live oaks add to the variety of form and texture.

Throughout the seven miles of drives there are large plantings of azaleas, wisterias of several colors, camellias, cacti, magnolias, and palms. There are numerous parking areas from which walking paths lead to points of special interest. One of these is the sunken garden which fills a deep-dish hollow with green growth to whose dramatic, dark beauty the blossom color is secondary.

The bayou and bayou lagoon islands are enriched by huge, ivory-white sago palm blossoms under which ducks, geese, and swans waddle and paddle. From the bayou is a startling view of a Chinese Pagoda Temple standing high on a stone cairn. To accept its invitation to be viewed close up is to see an authentic Temple Buddha housed inside. It was built by Chou Ha Chin in the 11th Century for Shoufa Temple northeast of Peking at the order of Emperor Hui Tsung. The temple was looted by a warlord general who sent his booty to New York to be sold at auction. Friends of the gardens' founder heard of the shipment's contents and, in 1936, bought the Buddha as a gift to the garden. On a tablet below the Temple are these words by E. A. McIlhenny:

Buddha Speaks

Peacefully I rest upon this lagoon's bank
As pale green bamboos sway above my throne.
Clouds of blossoms soften the sifted light
Falling golden and misty through the boughs above.
Long days of travel brought me from my home,
Yet I have known no hour of calmer rest.
My thoughts are like the swaying bamboos's crest
Waved to and fro above the rippling stream,
Clear and blue as from a glorious dream.

Buddha Temple stands on its own eminence above the bayou waters.

213

The Sunken Garden at Avery is thick with tropical growth.

The intricate drives lead, finally, to the hill above the pond and marsh first seen at the beginning. Few visitors fail to stop and go down again to the lookout tower to watch the graceful white birds at rest and in flight.

These flocks exist because of E. A. McIlhenny's personal conservation efforts to save the once threatened species. M'sieu Ned, as he was familiarly known, was told by a British Viceroy to India of a Rajah who had, for the delight of his young Ranee, constructed bamboo cages large enough to permit flight within by the exotic birds there confined. The birds nested, mated, and reared their young within these huge cages. After the Rajah's death the cages were neglected and deteriorated but the birds which had been hatched and reared there remained though they were no longer forcibly contained, and they raised broods of their own.

In the spring of 1892, M'sieu Ned built a "flying cage" of wire over part of the artificial lake on Avery Island. He himself went into the swamps and captured seven young snowy egrets, put them in the cage, fed them, watched them grow to maturity, and saw them select mates, build nests, hatch, and rear their young. At the beginning of the next migratory season, he destroyed the cage and watched the egrets fly off to South America. The next spring, he saw the same birds return to the place of their one-time confinement. The nesting, breeding, migration, and return have been repeated over all the years till, now, the birds are so numerous that each year truckloads of twigs for nesting material are dumped around Bird City to provide an adequate supply for the 20,000 nests the herons build each February.

By early July the nestlings are on their own. The adult birds fly out over the marsh waterways to seek their food, leaving the Bird City lake for the young birds' feeding. During the nesting time, several large alligators cruise around the lake discouraging predators who might otherwise swim out and rob the egrets' nests. In March the alligators' young may be observed on the shore areas.

After leaving the gardens most visitors make one more stop on Avery Island, to see the McIlhenny Tabasco Sauce enterprise. The sauce is made from fiercely hot Mexican peppers grown on the Island. It is the basis for part of the fortune which built the gardens. The other half derived from the mining of salt which is the bedrock of Avery. The basic condiments—pepper and salt—were parlayed by a great, visionary man into the wherewithal to finance an important conservation and horticultural work.

11th Century Chinese Buddha sits in untroubled contemplation on Avery Island.

Hodges
Many, Louisiana

Louisiana's Sabine and Vernon Parishes are a change from the flat, open marshland of the Bayou country. Low, rolling hills are heavily forested with pine as they were before 1900.

The first twenty years of this century were not kind to this land as quick-money lumbermen cut and ran, stripping away its green flesh and leaving amputated stumps and broken limbs to mark their depredations.

Some men and women restore homes and gardens; some restore old things; others, such as George W. Vanderbilt in North Carolina, Cason Callaway in Georgia, and A. J. Hodges in Louisiana, restore the land. Hodges was a successful oilman with a strong interest in the conservation of natural resources. He realized that when a barrel of oil was extracted from the ground there was one less barrel left and no way to restore or replace it; but mature trees could properly be harvested while new growth was planted and maintained as replacement for that cut down. So feeling, he turned his attention to the reforestation of more than 100,000 acres of wasted land and became an outstanding lumberman whose work furthered his conservation ideals.

In his reforestation experiments Hodges selected an east to west ridge of the Kisatchie Hills for an arboretum where hybridizing experiments were carried on to develop a crossbreed pine for straightness and toughness. Within the 4700 acres of the arboretum was an abandoned stone quarry abounding in wild flowers, lichen-covered rock, and seedling pines. Mr. Hodges quickly saw that this natural beauty had remarkable potential as a woodland garden and began developing it using what already existed as his guide. He said, "There never was an overall plan or drawing for the Gardens as a whole. Cleaning up and arranging one section naturally called for the opening and arranging of an adjoining section. Walks were laid where it was felt one would naturally stroll through the area. Bridges were built over depressions where water would run after a heavy rain. Steps were placed where you would want to climb from one level to another. Hardly a rock was moved, and never—no never—a worthwhile tree cut down."

The outcroppings of rock, the various levels, even the roadbed of the old tram railway were the basic ingredients of which the gardens were built. However, it is characteristic of the land restorers that they exercise their strong creative proclivities and Hodges was no exception. He created, in addition to a garden, a dam, a 225-acre lake, cascading streams, and an animal haven where deer and elk thrive.

The ridge tops one of the highest elevations in Louisiana. From it, to the west, Texas may be seen across the pine tops and Toledo Bend Lake. It was once part of Spanish Texas whose first capital, Las Adais, was just fifteen miles to the north on El Camino Real (the King's Highway).

To the right of the drive to the gardens lies a forty-foot-long petrified tree trunk which was dug out when the dam core was being prepared nearby. In moving it from the place where it lay intact for thousands of years, it was broken into several pieces. It has been placed in the Lauraceae family, of the genus Persea and may be an ancestor to the present day avocado.

Another unusual remnant of the past may be seen in the Natural Scenic area. It is the stump and root structure of a longleaf pine, almost impervious to rot because of the oleoresins or pitch throughout its heart and root section. The roots of the longleaf pine usually grow straight down and to comparatively great depth especially in dry, sandy soil. In this rocky ground, however, the roots grew around the underground rock formations. This tree was cut in early 1919. It was estimated to have been over three hundred years old and yielded over three thousand board feet of high-quality lumber.

Longleaf pine stump is almost impervious to rot. This giant is estimated to have been over 300 years old when it was felled.

It is kept as a reminder of the improper timbering practices followed when it was felled without thought or action to replace it with a new generation.

One of the most delightful things about Hodges is the opportunity to see the components of the garden from several aspects. Each of the levels may be viewed close-up, at eye level; they may also be seen from below or from above. Rocks, plantings, blooms, streams, cascades, and pools, individually and in combination, reflect varying characteristics when viewed from different elevations.

Miles of drives lead past the features of Hodges Gardens. The rose gardens occupy a slope above the open-air theater at the lake shore. Out on the lake, where fishermen cast for bass, a man-made geyser breaks the placid surface of the water. Around the lake, on one of three islands, is a flag-adorned structure built as a memorial to the Louisiana Purchase. The floor is a giant terrazzo map of the forty-eight contiguous States with the acquisition area of the Purchase defined. The nineteen poles fly five of the ten governmental standards which have flown over Louisiana and the flags of the thirteen states carved out of the land bought from France. The nineteenth flag is that of Hodges Gardens.

The broad sweeps of open land are grazed by a herd of forty elk within a fenced area and, roaming at large, five hundred to seven hundred head of deer of six varieties. Recreational facilities, motel and food accommodations all meet the high standards of Hodges but they are subordinated to the gardens and the forest.

In 1965, Hodges was presented the "Project Earth Award" and, in 1966, the year of his death, he received the "Silver Seal" award for his contributions as a conservationist and creator of beauty by the National Council of State Garden Clubs, Inc.

Hodges' associates are carrying forward his idea that "the Gardens will probably never be finished," that improvements can and must continue to be made while seeking unattainable perfection. That goal may well be unattainable but Hodges Gardens is not far away from perfection.

Birds-eye views give Hodges another dimension elsewhere not often appreciated by man.

ALABAMA

Hamilton-Smith House
Mobile, Alabama

In 1968, Mrs. Edwin K. Smith who had lived along the Dog River until Col. Smith died, bought and restored the Hamilton House to what it had been when it was constructed about 120 years ago. The outer walls of old hand-fashioned brick are of a distinctive color set off by the mortar which joins them. This mortar, made of white sand and ground oyster shells is ivory white in contrast to the pink, red and brown bricks. The inside of the house retains all the characteristics of Mobile architecture. The ceilings are very high as are the doorways whose framings were modeled after the columns at Luxor. This Egyptian theme is seen in many old Mobile homes. In the main sitting room the ceilings are decorated with elaborate plaster rosettes from which are suspended French crystal chandeliers of exquisite workmanship and quality.

The garden is enclosed on two sides by the house and its extension. The other two sides are enclosed by a brick wall of medium height. The gates are of lovely lace ironwork, another much used medium of decoration and function in Mobile exteriors. This lacework is repeated in the wall ventilation openings and the upper balustrades. The columns of the garden gates are capped by the pineapple symbols of hospitality, and they do not lie.

Originally, this was a sunken garden whose level Mrs. Smith had raised about two feet to bring it into a better relationship with the house, the garden sitting room and the breakfast room. The effect of a sunken garden is retained but now there is a feeling that these parts of the house are one with the garden.

The enclosed area is about 45 x 70 feet but several things create an illusion of greater size. There is a splendid use of espaliered growth and use of background material which makes for a variegated foliage texture and color without causing shade. All around the house and garden is open space which lets in maximum light unobstructed by other buildings or trees.

To the rear, across the wide street, is the new Mobile Municipal Center and to the left across the wall is the Malaga Plaza.

Within the brick paved garden there are two major focal points—a delicately graceful cherry laurel and a palm which is more than a century old. The fountain statue of Sappho, the Greek poetess, looks out on the poetry of nature's words composed by a contemporary woman, Mrs. Smith. Behind Sappho grows another Egyptian touch, a planting of bullrushes such as those which hid the infant Moses. Two other statues represent spring and summer. Spring is in terra cotta, contrasting with the lead gray and bronze of the Sappho and summer pieces.

Garden wall ventilation is given beauty by the use of ironwork.

Bellingrath, Alabama

Smith House, Alabama

Jungle Gardens, Louisiana

Bellingrath, Alabama

Bellingrath, Alabama

Clumps of calendula bring a winter note of yellow and pale green brightness. Potted maidenhair fern is an important part of the vocabulary of this poem. Great beds of Michaelmas daisies sing a gay song through much of the year. A large Philippine jar of bronze color is a reminder of the extensive travels Col. and Mrs. Smith enjoyed during his military career. The international background of the garden is shared with its neighbor across the wall.

The Spanish Plaza is a copy of a garden in Malaga, Mobile's counterpart city in Spain. In Malaga is a Mobile Plaza. The Spanish Plaza has been placed as a great fronting for the Municipal Center. It extends across Church Street and covers another full block in addition to the section next to the Smith house.

Among the gifts to Mobile from Malaga is a replica of the official symbol of that city, a statue of "El Cenachero," the basket carrier, or fishmonger. The original stands in Mobile Park in Malaga. At the opposite end of the plaza is another splendid gift, a statue of Isabel la Catolica which stood in the Spanish Pavilion at the New York World's Fair. Its pedestal houses the only replica of the crown and scepter of Queen Isabella. The originals lie in the royal chapel of Granada.

The design of the great fountain was inspired by famous fountains of Spain. Half-circling the fountain are eleven friendship arches and the colorful flags given by the ten provinces visited by Mobile's Cultural and Historic Mission to Spain—the provinces which exerted the greatest influence on Spanish exploration and culture on the Gulf Coast.

Glass mosaics around the fountain pictorialize the most beautiful or most famous buildings and monuments of each of Spain's 53 provinces as determined by each provincial parliament.

There are twelve ceramic tile benches, each depicting an historic vista with landmark monuments from the cities represented.

A statue of Alfonse X (the Wise) faces one of Bernardo de Galvez, born in Malaga in 1746. Galvez captured Mobile for the Spanish and began 33 years of Spanish rule. He served as Governor of the Territory of Louisiana.

Mobile was founded by the French, taken by the British, then by the Spanish, was part of the Republic of Alabama, was part of the Confederacy and, in 1865, was restored to the Union. Mobile calls itself "the city of six flags" since, over the years, six different flags have flown over it. It is now a city of live-oak lined streets and lacy ironwork, a symbol of a South turned from agriculture to industry, from slavery to freedom, from seccession to unity. It has not, however, turned from its air of gentility and grace.

Statue of Queen Isabella which stood in the Spanish Pavilion at the New York World's Fair.

225

The Spanish Plaza is a copy of a garden in Malaga, Spain.

Bellingrath Gardens
Theodore, Alabama

Bellingrath reflects taste, imagination and attention to detail which result in near perfection in each of the many aspects which give so much variety to this "Charm Spot of the Deep South."

There is a long, gentle, winding drive to the reception building. It is an introduction to the impeccability of the whole place.

Entry to the gardens is made through a covered mall resplendent at all times with seasonal plantings.

Under an arched bridge there is the first view of the great, circular rose garden. Its design was created to pay tribute to the Rotary Club in which Mr. Bellingrath had a long-time interest. The pools of the rose garden are graced by day-flowering, tropical water lilies.

The open rock garden boasts thousands of African violets growing outdoors in the bland climate of the Gulf Coast. Rocks play an important part all through Bellingrath Gardens. They are artfully arranged to give the impression that they are a natural part of their present location, but they were all brought here from many miles away.

The Exotica Conservatory is aptly named for its display of exotic tropical growth of extensive variety. Here one may see the tree fern with its palm-like trunk and fern-like fronds gracefully draped overhead.

Down a winding walk rich with deep greens and brilliant blossom is a brick patio which looks out on the expansive bulb beds that border the sweep of the great lawn through whose tree-lined far border the first sight of the gracious brick house filters between leaves and branches.

The Camellia Parterre is only one of several Bellingrath areas featuring this belle of Southern blossoms. The parterre leads directly to the pool at one end of which stands Rebecca at the Well. Leading from the pool is a canal whose far extremity displays the Mermaid Fountain.

At the left is an island in the courtyard whose brilliant planting dramatizes the Monolith bearing the history of the Gardens.

To the right of the courtyard is the south terrace of ballast slate paving divided by a waterway whose waters spill out over the Grotto where plantings are changed with the seasons. The drama of the Grotto is sensational but it must share attention with the view of the Ile-aux-Oies River and marshes. Silvery, river fish splash in the water below the retaining wall that leads to the boathouse that stands as a reminder that this was a simple fishing camp before becoming a garden.

All of the rocks at Bellingrath had to be brought from hundreds of miles away.

A rising walk first comes around to the North Terrace, a secluded spot which affords a splendid view of the river and then continues around the house built around a sunken garden radiant with year-round bloom. Through its loggia arches, the beauty of the century-old lacework iron trim of the balcony repeats leaf and flower of the growing plants beneath.

Across the courtyard is the building which houses an exhibit of man-made birds and flowers sculptured and glazed by the great American artist, Edward Marshall Boehm, who has done in porcelain what Audubon did through drawings and engravings. The medium of porcelain in the hands of Boehm has given to the world a full-dimension representation of the flora and fauna of this haven at Bellingrath. The translucence of the paper-thin porcelain is so like the translucence of flower petal and outspread wing that many viewers ask whether these are real birds and flowers. On occasion, members of the staff do "put on" the questioners by explaining that the plants are so delicate that they must be grown behind protective glass.

Edward Boehm perfected his formula for hard paste porcelain in 1950. He was the first American to successfully work in this medium originated over 2000 years ago by the Chinese. The colors for the glazes were hand ground by Boehm's ceramists. That this great collection of 86 pieces ranging in size from a few inches to the seven-foot centerpiece, the Ivory-billed Woodpecker, is housed at Bellingrath is a wonderful complement to the life outside. Its greatest value is in its beauty, but its monetary value, immense during the artist's life, is made immeasurably greater since his premature death at the age of 53.

The walk around Mirror Lake leads to a path to the North Bayou observation platform where the tidewater flow of the inlet may be seen close at hand. Deer feed directly below. Waterfowl cruise the surface. Along this path is a grove of tree-high bamboo which grows to its full height within 30 days from shooting up new canes. Along the way is the large Camellia Arboretum covering acres of this species in great variety.

Places to rest are provided at a terraced view of the rockery across the water. A little way along are the bubbling pool and the bridge under whose arch swim braces of white swans.

For many, the Oriental-American Garden is the highlight of Bellingrath. It combines oriental and occidental traditions in a happy marriage. The first vista, in three directions from the benched terrace, extends an invitation for closer viewing along the many paths and bridges and stepping-stones that traverse water and sloping land. Just below the terrace flamingoes preen and fluff their pink plumage. Rock and monkey grass lined paths open new perspectives on what has already been seen and reveal hidden glories around the bends. A charming little Japanese teahouse is reached across circular stepping-stones imprinted with impressions of *Fatsia Japonica* leaves.

Each of the bridges in the garden is individual in design, the largest being the exquisitely arched half-moon bridge.

The entire garden is enclosed by a reed and bamboo wall which frames several Torii gates. The gate across from the first terrace bears a circular red sign with white Japanese letters. Translated, it reads, "Drink Coca-Cola." The fortune used to create all this loveliness was derived from a Coca-Cola bottling franchise.

Displayed in places which will best show their beauty are many oriental garden objects. Wind chimes tinkle in the breeze and birds sing songs which say beauty in any language.

Through the gate, under the owl lantern, and down the path over the bridge under which entry was made, past the unusual variety of pyracantha with its angular forms and red berries is the reception building where flower paintings by Louise Estes are on display. These watercolors depict the various blooms and leaves of Bellingrath.

They are the products of love, genius and patience. It is to be hoped that their creator, an insufficiently recognized and under-valued artist will soon gain the renown and reward her great talent deserves.

Bellingrath Gardens are now operated by the Bellingrath-Morse Foundation set up in 1950 by Walter D. Bellingrath. In the preamble to the Deed of Trust he wrote: "In the evening of our lives my beloved wife, Bessie Morse Bellingrath, and I found untold pleasure and happiness in the development of the Gardens which bear our name. During the past decade thousands of our fellow citizens have enjoyed the rare and lovely spectacle which nature, with our help, has provided in this charm spot of the deep South. The inspiration which we received as we carried on our work of developing the Gardens and the pleasant and appreciative reaction of the many visitors to the Gardens resulted in plans for the perpetuation of this beauty, so that those who come after us may visit the Gardens and enjoy them. In working out our plans, it occurred to us that the operation of the Gardens could be carried on in a way that would continue their existence and yet fulfill another worthy objective of ours. To this end, I am providing herein that the income from the operation of the Gardens be devoted to the intellectual and religious upbringing of young men and women of our Southland, as well as to foster and perpetuate those Christian values which were recognized by our forefathers as

A close-up view of the Grotto in Bellingrath Gardens. It overlooks the Ile-aux-Oise River and is maintained with seasonal flowers and plants the year 'round.

*The high arch of the half-moon bridge frames the
reflection of the trees and wall beyond.*

essential for the building of a great nation."
The beneficiaries are Southwestern of
Memphis; Huntingdon College,
Montgomery, Alabama; Stillman College
(a Presbyterian College for black students),
Tuscaloosa, Alabama; the Central
Presbyterian Church and St. Francis Street
Methodist Church, both of Mobile.

A final note which indicates the thoroughness of the hospitality and consideration
which guide Bellingrath is the following:
"located near the entrance building is a
free Pet Motel which provides comfortable
quarters for pets while their masters visit the
Gardens and Home." Seeing-eye dogs
accompanying their blind masters are the
only pets permitted inside the Gardens.
The operators of Bellingrath realize that
some visitors planning a brief stay might
leave pets in cars and then, succumbing
to the lure of the place, stay longer than
they had intended, leaving the pets in
unpleasant, unattended confinement. Even
pets are assured a joyful stay at Bellingrath
Gardens.

Flamingoes live happily in the Oriental-American section. They are not fenced in and can roam wherever they please but prefer to stay in this one area.

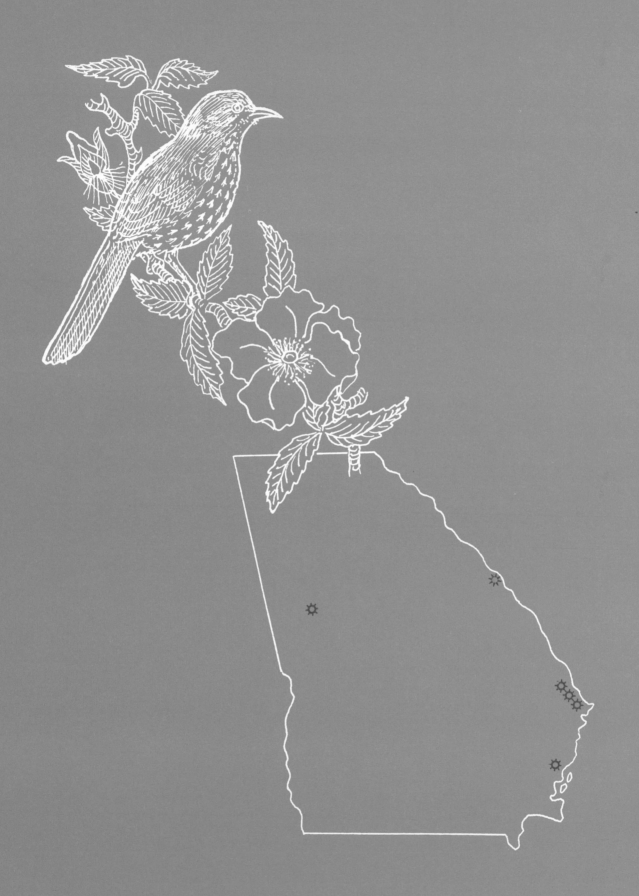

GEORGIA

Mrs. Bolton Duffield
Sea Island, Georgia

Unusual on Sea Island, famous in the past for long staple cotton, is the Japanese style architecture of Mrs. Bolton Duffield's home, located on a bluff overlooking sea marshes. The siting of the house on a slope next to a large, spreading live oak dictated the form and style of house and garden, which could be called "modified oriental" in theme and character. As do all good Japanese style buildings, the house takes its place beautifully as a natural part of its surroundings.

In her gardens Mrs. Duffield has used the form and feeling of Japanese gardens without locking herself into copying or duplicating and without tying herself to the use of symbolism for symbolism's sake. The guiding—and she emphasizes "guiding" —principle of the East which inspired her is that nature rather than man should determine planting and design. Multiple curves lend not only grace but bring about the existence of "surprise" areas and isolated statements of containment within the whole. Reverse perspective principles are used to bring specific dramatic forms, shapes and colors of some distant plants closer to the visual consciousness while creating the illusion of added space and distance by using soft, diffused textures as backgrounds.

The living room of the house is really an observation room of glass enclosed space from which the rise and fall of sea water in the marshes may be seen as an integral part of the garden plan which employs, in its lower areas, a pool created by tidewater. The incoming tides bring silvery fingerlings dancing on and through the flow which, at high water, surrounds most of the house.

Wind-gnarled cedars at the garden edge provide naturally created forms similar to Japanese man-formed shapes. Low growing shore juniper with its jagged texture grows down to the piling set to contain the pool water. These shapes are in contrast to the curves of the garden walks. At one spot tall piling forms a large loop "s" whose design

grace also functions as a container for the compost heap which supplies this organic garden.

The garden paths are of gravel rather than of oyster shell which is widely used on the Golden Isles. The entry way paving does employ "tabby," a local form of cement and oyster shell mix which is virtually indestructible and impervious to attack by salt air and water.

Fenced against the encroachments of native deer is a vegetable and herb garden which meets the household needs. Fig trees supply needed shade from summer sun and give a bounty of luscious fruit.

The out of doors is brought into the house more than visually in the form of an indoor garden court at the front entrance. It is a continuation of the garden which grows under the living room wing. The ground slopes down to face an afternoon sun that warms and lights the ground cover planting of ivy. From almost anywhere in the house there is an awareness of the live oak's outstretched arms seeming to be giving a blessing to everything it guards.

The graceful curves of the piling enclosure create a design motif while, at the same time, containing the compost heap.

At night, the exterior is softly lit so that even in the hours of dark the garden may be enjoyed from within and the sense of oneness of interior and exterior may be maintained. The variety of growth separated by multiple winding paths and the vista of the marshes bordered in the distance by trees give a quality of expansive limitlessness to the basic intimacy of this small garden.

While this is the creation and the work of Mrs. Duffield she has benefitted from consultation with a young landscape architect, Elwin Sasser, member of the firm headed by the great T. M. Baumgartner.

This is an American garden which has taken its lessons and beauty from American ground, space and flora, and the disciplines of oriental gardening free of undue strictures.

Virtually all of the flowering takes place in an abbreviated spring season. Bulbs, cherry and peach blossoms, white azaleas, white oleanders, and weeping cherry offer restrained notes of color in a garden conceived to bring green, textured beauty around the year. In the autumn, two cypresses turn brilliant orange and accent the front view of the property. The marshes, green in spring and summer, gold in autumn, and tawny gray in winter change the color harmonies as they tell the change of season. It is entirely coincidental that as there are 17 syllables in a haiku poem there are 17 individual areas in this garden.

Entry to house shows the compatibility achieved between garden, house, and surroundings.

Each of the seventeen garden areas has its own charm
and natural quality which flows from one to the next.

Gas lanterns add to the charm of the Trustees' Garden walks. Liriope lines the magnolia shaded brick walks which lead from one part of the Trustees' Garden to another.

beauty that was neither buried nor pirated by industrial development or urban "modernization."

The feel of the area may be sensed from the seat of a car but it is most thoroughly appreciated by walking through the streets and the squares. Almost as though he foresaw the need to reduce pollution-exhaling automotive traffic Oglethorpe designed a city in which everything can comfortably be reached on foot. Buildings, streets and squares form a total area of which each component is a positive, contributing part of the whole.

Edmund N. Bacon's book *Design of Cities* is a study of twenty-two of the world's great cities. Savannah is one. Of Oglethorpe's plan, Bacon writes, "It is amazing that a colony, struggling against the most elemental problems of survival in a wilderness, should be able to produce a plan so exalted that it remains as one of the finest diagrams for city organization and growth in existence." Basically, the plan called for a one-acre square of public garden surrounded by eight narrow blocks and four very small blocks, all forming a cellular square component, to be repeated again and again as expansion needs required.

Each of the squares has its own character which extends to the surrounding blocks which comprise the square's unit. While these individualities, expressive of the specific time of development, are evident, they do not interrupt the continuity which flows from square to square to square. There is an unbroken tranquility in Savannah that is rare in contemporary urban life.

Along the water front which is the northerly border of Historic Savannah are Emmett Park and the Strand. The southern border is marked by the 30-acre Forsyth Park. The eastern border is what once was The Trustees' Garden, America's first experimental agricultural garden. Its ten acres were used for the study and development of cotton, fruit trees, vineyards and mulberries for silk production. The silk and wine industries failed to materialize but

the seed from the cotton provided the base for the South's pre-Civil War economy and the textile-based economy of the North. The fruit trees that emanated from this garden spread through the southeast and made the words "Georgia Peach" synonymous with excellence. In the 1750s the Trustees' Garden became Savannah's first urban fatality when the land was subdivided as an easy answer to the need for expanded residential space. A substantial part of this section was later acquired by the Savannah Gas Company whose "holder" (tank) dominates the scene.

The east side of East Broad Street from St. Julian to Broughton St., standing in the shadow of the monstrous gas storage tank, is the old residential property now owned and maintained by the company. The houses are next to the famous Pirate's House and Herb House with their blue shutters which, in early days, were believed to ward off evil spirits. Today, it is all a lovely restoration of early houses and gardens which have the charm of a fine, old patchwork quilt. The gas lamps that give night time illumination add greatly to the atmosphere of age which in one way diminishes and, in another way, emphasizes the anachronistic presence of the tank.

These gas-lit gardens contain many of the original herbs and plants once grown in the Trustees' Garden of the 1730s and 1740s. This, Savannah's first large restoration project set the tone for succeeding restoration efforts in Historic Savannah. It demonstrates what responsible, essential industry can do to reduce the esthetic damage its presence usually causes. What has been done here, however, also emphasizes the ugliness of this industry's principal structure and brings into sharp focus the need for additional effort.

The walls of the several gardens, instead of dividing them, are like the stitches of a quilt which hold the pieces together in a familial unity in which individuality is maintained without sacrifice of kinship. The gardens range in size from modest to small to tiny except for a community area of open lawn. In January, a row of red buds unselfishly brightens its own and the neighboring gardens with its profusion of fuchsia pink blossoms.

In addition to Savannah's parks and squares, many of its streets have wide center malls running their lengths. Traffic flow, because of one-way streets, flows smoothly past and around the squares. Some of the squares are bisected by dirt lanes that facilitate the movement of large fire-fighting equipment.

Row buildings are the basic architectural theme of Savannah. It leaves little space for private gardens but there is a much reduced need for these because of the planning which created public gardens to serve the community. Tourists must recognize that the primary emphasis is on the 1100 buildings of architectural note. There is enough horticultural beauty in the squares and along the walks to satisfy the greatest appetite.

Rushing and high pressure living is completely out of key with the relaxed atmosphere which leads businessmen, after a leisurely lunch, to say, "Let's take a walk; it will do us good." Strollers enjoy a fine day with all their senses, seeing the beauty, smelling the fresh air, feeling the caress of soft breezes, hearing the sounds of birds and rustling leaves, tasting the pleasure of tranquility. All of this in an urban setting gives Savannah the right to be considered by experts one of the finest city plans ever developed.

Washington Square.

Chippewa Square houses Savannah's most . . . distinguished statue, a bronze figure of James Edward Oglethorpe, facing southward to commemorate his victory over the Spanish in 1742. . . . . . .

This small garden is an excellent representative of the way in which great beauty may be achieved simply in limited space. It is only one of the many gardens of Augusta which calls itself "the Garden City of the South."

As the home of the Augusta National Golf Course where annually the Masters Tournament is played during the height of the spring blooming season Augusta plays boniface to many tourists who can enjoy, as they drive to and from the Golf Course, the beauty of many gardens.

The walls of old brick feature scratched mortar joints. The walls are partially covered with fig vine and espaliered *camellia sassanqua* at whose feet are white azaleas. Heavily pruned Carolina cherry gives a change of form and texture to the wall planting. The walls themselves are designed as a series of panels which function as a sectional divider with walk throughs that provide both access and ventilation. Such walls become an integral part of the garden rather than just serving as a limits marker.

Fences with closed gates emphasize the intimate privacy of many Augusta gardens.

Slopes of the Augusta hills make ideal display areas for azaleas which flourish in the August climate.

Callaway Gardens
Pine Mountain, Georgia

Callaway Gardens is the story of a cycle begun in the remotest reaches of time past on the oldest land of the continent—red soil made rich through countless millennia, robbed of its richness by man's misuse, and re-created by a man who worked as an instrument of God with money earned from the very crop which depleted the earth's fertility.

"The best fertilizer a land can have is the footprint of its owner." These are the words of Cason Callaway, who left his indelible impress on the 2500 acres of Pine Mountain called Callaway Gardens. This once fertile land had been almost destroyed by a relatively few generations of cotton cropping. Callaway felt money earned on cotton could best be spent to replenish the richness of this red Georgia earth.

In 1938, at the age of 44, he resigned from the Callaway Mills to devote the rest of his life to the work he assigned himself—to make "not just the finest garden seen on earth since Adam was a boy but the prettiest garden that will be seen on earth till Gabriel blows his horn."

On 30,000 acres of worn out farmlands and cut-over forests Callaway filled in the gullies of eroded hillsides and drained the silt-clogged bottom lands. Resolved never to plant a stalk of cotton, he experimented with a hundred different crops, vegetable, avian and piscean. Much of what he did presaged current ecological conservation efforts. The work drew visitors from all over the country. One visitor said, "Cason, this just goes to show what God could do if he had money." It was a humorous but unfair remark since Callaway was not, as some other men of wealth have done, playing God. He was humbly, but resolutely, giving back what man had taken from the soil and striving to find ways to maintain the restored productivity through proper farming. He was a leading apostle of financial help to poor, small farmers who were caught in a trap of intensifying impoverishment which held both the farmer and his land.

The concept for the Gardens came from Callaway's farming experiments. On abandoned, gullied hilltop farms he put men and equipment to work. Along the clear creek he built dams of water-impervious clay to create a chain of eleven lakes. To keep the lake beds silt-free he built a six-mile diversion ditch to carry storm-borne run-off waters and he paved the lake-connecting streams with fieldstone to trap silt and keep the lakes clear.

His first thoughts were to make a place where old friends could come to visit or to live in congenial surroundings. These thoughts soon changed. He realized that wealthy retirees could go anywhere they wanted to find beauty and relaxation, but a hardware clerk, a shoe salesman or a factory worker had virtually no place to go to take his family for a happy weekend or quiet vacation in beautiful surroundings. He decided to fill that void. He said: "Before we built the gardens here, if a man wanted to take his family on a picnic, the best place he could find was a cut-over forest of pine stumps. If he wanted to take his kids swimming all that was available was a muddy frog pond. All I've done is to try to fix it so that anybody who came here would see something beautiful wherever he might look. I don't know what the soul is, but whatever it is, a sense of beauty and good-ness must be at the heart of it."

Geologists say that Pine Mountain is the oldest land on the American continent—the tail bone of the Appalachian Range. A few places, too steep for farming and too rugged for sawmillers, survived man's depredations and the natural beauty remained as an example of what all of Pine Mountain had been. One such place, Blue Springs, was found by Mr. and Mrs. Callaway and they acquired it for a summer place. Here, Mr. Callaway found a flower he had never seen before. His wife identified it as the

Ducks swim past the blossoms on the water lily pond at Callaway.

Rhododendron Pruniflorium Azalea, a midsummer bloomer found only within a 100-mile radius of the Blue Springs. Callaway's decision to insure its preservation led to his first conservation efforts. Today, this azalea is the visual identification symbol of Callaway Gardens.

The rough dirt road at Blue Springs was difficult for visitors to traverse so it was paved. A stranger, following this then new road pulled up in front of the log house and called to Callaway, "Hey Mister, where does this road go?" "Mexico City," was the straight-faced answer. "No it don't," the man said. "Yes it does," Callaway replied. "If I was going to leave here to go to Mexico City that's the road I'd take."

Another day, a family of trespassers was picnicking by the private lake. Mr. Callaway went down to berate the strangers. "What can I do for you, sir?" he asked the man. "Well," the man said pleasantly, "you might get us some crackers for the baby." Callaway did and invited the people to enjoy their picnic. Such were the seeds which, sown in a fertile mind, grew and blossomed finally into the idea of creating a great garden for people to enjoy.

One of the frequent visitors to the Callaway home was President Franklin D. Roosevelt with whom Callaway "disagreed fundamentally on all the fundamentals." Nonetheless, there was between the men mutual respect and fondness which often brought the President from nearby Warm Springs to visit and relax.

"Recreation and re-creation" were the guide words which determined the design course of the garden and its attendant recreational facilities. Thousands of tons of white sand were brought in to make the biggest inland man-made sand beach in the world. Bath houses were built to accommodate 3000 people. Golf courses were laid out around lakes and woods. Vacation cottages were built. Tennis courts were created. Bridle paths and cycling roads were provided. Lakes were stocked for fishing. A big, open shed with a barbecue pit was erected for family reunion and Sunday School picnic use. House boats and small paddle boats were put on the water for relaxed cruising or drifting. A spectator pavilion for the viewing of water ski competition was built. Driving trails through the garden acres were paved and natural walking trails were carved to lead through the various areas. Grounds were specially planted to attract birds. Wild flower sections—botanical gardens each featuring different varieties in their natural settings—can be enjoyed on foot, or bicycle or from a car. There are resting places for observation or contemplation. At the entry points of several of the sections folders or brochures identifying and describing the growth of the area are put out for the taking.

There is only one somewhat formal garden where chrysanthemums and seasonal blooms are displayed to maximum advantage near the greenhouse and conservatory. In this garden are the only fountains to be found at Callaway though there are plenty of streams and waterfalls running natural courses through the woods.

Even the simplest wild flowers moved from the deeper woods are treated with the care and affection a specialist would lavish on a rare cultivated specimen. "You can put a ten-cent flower in a fifty-cent hole and it will live and grow and thrive," Cason Callaway said. "But if you put a fifty-cent flower in a ten-cent hole it will die." The horticultural success of the Gardens attests to the wisdom of this philosophy.

Because he felt that most people today have little opportunity to see many fruits and vegetables growing, Callaway planned the unique 7½ acre Fruit, Vegetable and Berry Garden. He wanted to make use of the knowledge he had gained in his earlier agricultural experiments to develop a fine demonstration garden which can guide visitors to better select the kinds of fruits and vegetables which would be best in their own gardens. Today, "Mr. Cason's Vegetable Garden" provides much of the succulent,

Ida Cason Callaway Memorial Chapel of stone is a place for inter-faith meditation and contemplation.

fresh produce served at the tables of the clubhouse and inn dining rooms—making it easier to keep everything about Callaway "genuine." The fare served at the inn is genuine, bountiful and delicious.

Callaway Gardens was named as a memorial to Ida Cason Callaway, Cason's mother. To complete the memorial he planned the Chapel which is one of the many highlights of the gardens and approved its design before his death in 1961. Slate-roofed, fieldstone-walled, arched with timbers hewn from the surrounding hills, the Chapel stands beside a natural waterfall at the head of a small lake. It is a Chapel for meditation or prayer in a place ideal for either. Afternoon organ recitals regularly add a special grace to this quiet nook of nature. The marriages which are solemnized before the great natural stone that serves as an altar are the only religious services conducted in this Chapel intended for private contemplation. The magnificent stained glass windows tell, with nature's transmitted light, the story of a garden for all seasons as seen by a great artist in this difficult medium.

Thirty young members of the Florida State University Circus are brought to the Gardens for the summer. Not only do they perform their aerial acrobatic shows, but work with visiting children—teaching them water-skiing, group games, nature lore, and circus acrobatics. And they just talk with the kids about anything that is on the youngsters' minds.

There is a program of horticultural education and brochures are prepared and distributed which pass to average gardeners the knowledge of the specialists employed by the Gardens.

There are many facilities at Callaway; all maintain the devotion to excellence so clearly seen in the Gardens. All of the revenue derived from these satellite enterprises go directly toward the financing of the non-income producing projects that make Callaway a place of complete charm. They make it possible to keep Cason Callaway's realized dream an actuality.

Much of the preceding text was transcribed from the words spoken by Howard "Bo" Callaway about his father and the Gardens he built. In describing the complex man who was his father, Bo Callaway lists his practicality as a business executive, his artist's sensibility to beauty, his friendly warmth of spirit, his philanthropist's concern for his fellow man, and his ecologist's love of the land. Then he says, "It would be simpler, and more effective, to say to each of you, 'Go and see for yourself what the Gardens are.' Once you have done this you will know far more about Cason Callaway and the kind of man he was and the dream he lived to see come true than I could ever tell you. For it is clear to me that his more fitting eulogy is written in the trees and the flowers, in the lakes and the woodlands, and the green of open spaces, than in anything I might say about him."

It is typical of this family's dedication to public service that the Callaway Mills, a large and prospering textile enterprise is no longer operated for private gain. Through the instrumentality of a charitable foundation all its assets and earnings are dedicated to the support and enrichment of charitable and community enterprises.

This book closes with Callaway because anything else would be anticlimatic. It is an accomplishment of such great magnitude and natural grandeur, without a trace of ostentation, possessed of the reticence of its shy, delicate wild flowers, that it is a total expression of love of nature.

To so acknowledge Callaway's greatness is in no way to say that other gardens are less or inferior. It is simply a recognition that Callaway is *the* gem among gems.

Mrs. Duffield's Sea Island Garden is a haiku poem

The Elizabethan Gardens are a sonnet to Virginia Dare

Longue Vue, Bellingrath, Hodges, and Rosedown are splendid odes to beauty

Callaway is an epic to one man's love of nature.

Pioneer log cabin moved to Callaway to remind visitors of America's strong pioneer heritage.

The wise man returned to his simple home and quiet life. And although he was to serve the King many times afterward, the question of a reward never again arose.

The King ruled wisely and justly for many, many years, and to the end of his days he kept the chessboard with its thirty-two grains of rice to remind him of the wise man's lesson—how easy it is for pride to make a fool of anyone, even a king.

"Yes," said the King at last. "Yes, I am satisfied."

Then he smiled at the wise man, not a happy smile perhaps, but a genuine smile. "And I understand," the King said, "that in all this you have done me yet another service."

"Then, sire, I am truly rewarded," said the wise man. With that he bowed very low and left the great hall.

you, sire. I have always been satisfied. It was *you* who insisted on rewarding me. It is *you* who must be satisfied."

As the wise man spoke these words all the splendid people in the great hall became very, very still.

"*Are* you satisfied, sire?" asked the wise man. And although he spoke quietly, everyone heard him as if he had shouted. No one whispered. No one moved.

"This must stop," said the King to the wise man. "There is not enough rice in all of India to reward you."

"No, indeed, sire," said the wise man. "There is not enough rice in all the world."

"Then," said the King, "since I have promised you the impossible, I command you as my loyal subject to tell me how you will be satisfied."

"But I *am* satisfied, sire," said the wise man. "It is as I tried to tell

Below he saw a line of thirty-two wagons leaving the granaries and huge, happy crowds following them.

The King sighed. He placed a grain of rice on the thirty-second square of his chessboard and then gave orders to summon the wise man to the palace.

Finally the Queen left him alone with his anger and silence. There
he sat all that day and there he stayed all that night, dozing fitfully until
he was awakened by the first light of morning.

He sat and glared at his chessboard with its thirty-one grains of rice —thirty-one days since he insisted the wise man should be rewarded. After a time the Queen said to him, "You must ask the wise man to release you from your promise. It is the only thing to be done."

But the King seemed not to hear.

"Enough!" said the King. "Summon the royal mathematicians."

The mathematicians appeared and were ordered to determine how many tons of rice the King had in fact promised to the wise man. After an hour of calculating and recalculating, the Chief Mathematician rather nervously held up a slate with their answer.

As the King read the number he grew angrier and angrier. "Five hundred forty-nine billion, seven hundred fifty-five million, eight hundred thirty thousand, eight hundred eighty-seven tons!

"Tons!" roared the King. "Tons! Deception and treason!" He then ordered everyone from his presence except the Queen.

On the day after that, when the King returned, he heard a great cheering outside his palace. From his window he saw sixteen wagons, each carrying sixteen sacks of rice—over a ton on each wagon. The wagons were followed by a crowd of happy people.

"Where are those wagons going?" the King demanded.

"Sire," said the Grand Superintendent of the King's Granaries, "that is the rice being sent today to the wise man."

"Impossible!" said the King. "You have made some mistake!"

"I fear not, sire," said the Grand Superintendent, and began to explain how one grain became two, then one ounce became two ounces, then a pound became—

But there had been no mistake.

It was explained how one grain became two and then four; grains became ounces; ounces became pounds; a bag became two bags; and today it was four sacks, each weighing one hundred twenty-eight pounds.

The Grand Superintendent said to himself, "Tomorrow there will be eight sacks—over half a ton! I must tell the King!"

But the King was away hunting in the mountains that day and the next. So on the following day the Grand Superintendent had to send the wise man over a ton of rice. The next day it was two tons. And still the King had not returned to the palace. There was nothing to be done....The next day four tons....Then eight tons.

It was only nine days later that the Grand Superintendent saw four granary workers carrying sacks of rice from the granary. Following them was a group of ragged children.

"Here! Stop!" shouted the Grand Superintendent. "Where are you going with the King's rice?"

When the children laughed at this, the Grand Superintendent demanded, "And why are these urchins so merry?"

"Your Excellency," said one of the granary workers, "we are carrying this rice to the wise man, who then gives it away to the poor and hungry."

"Impossible!" said the Grand Superintendent. "That fool of a Weigher has made some mistake."

But when he was actually standing before the Grand Superintendent, the Weigher became so nervous that he didn't say what he
meant to say.

"Your—Your Excellency," he stammered, "excuse me...the rice
sent to the wise man is...excuse me...How many small bags of rice are
there in the King's granaries?"

"What kind of question is that?" demanded the Grand Superintendent. "Weigher, have you been drinking?"

"N-no, Your Excellency," the Weigher said. Then he hurried back
to his scales and promised himself not to bother anybody again about
the wise man's rice.

But at the granaries the Weigher had become worried.

"Tomorrow," he said to himself, "it will be two one-pound bags, and the next day it will be four." He calculated the amounts: eight, sixteen, thirty-two.... When he got to two thousand forty-eight bags, he stopped in alarm. "I must tell the Grand Superintendent of the King's Granaries at once!"

Only four days later the wise man was sent a small bag of rice weighing sixteen ounces, or one pound. He placed one grain on the sixteenth square of his chessboard and gave the rest to a beggar.

The actual counting of the grains of rice was left to the Weigher of the King's Grain: two hundred fifty-six grains, then five hundred twelve, then one thousand twenty-four.

"Dear me," said the Weigher to himself on the twelfth day, "soon I'll be counting grains all day long." So instead of counting out two thousand forty-eight grains of rice, he simply weighed out an ounce of rice and sent it to the wise man.

On the eighth day there was no servant in splendid dress, but only an ordinary granary worker bringing one hundred twenty-eight grains of rice in a small pouch. The wise man placed one grain on the eighth square of his chessboard and threw the rest to a bird outside his window. By now the King had quite forgotten the wise man and his rice, and it was left to a servant to place a grain on the eighth square of the King's chessboard.

When the King heard this, he placed a grain of rice on the first square of his own chessboard.

On the second day two grains of rice were sent to the wise man, and the King and the wise man each placed a grain of rice on the second square of his chessboard. And so it went: four grains of rice to the wise man on the third day and a grain of rice on the third square, and so on.

To add to the humor the Grand Superintendent of the King's Granaries had a servant, wearing the most splendid garments, carry the first little grain of rice on a gleaming silver tray to the wise man's house. But the wise man merely thanked the servant and placed the grain on the first square of his chessboard.

Indeed, that would have been simple; but it would also have made it obvious to everyone that the King was not sure how much rice it was, and the King was too proud to let anyone think he was ever unsure of anything. So he did not ask the question. Instead, he smiled royally and said to the wise man, "Your complicated request is most simply granted."

This caused a stirring of laughter among the councillors and nobles, and as the wise man bowed and quietly left the hall, there was much amusement at this simple old man and his odd request.

Now the King wondered, as anyone would, just how many grains of rice this would be. He thought of grains of rice on a chessboard: one, two, four, eight, sixteen.... There were sixty-four squares. Would that be a pound of rice in all? The King wasn't sure.

At this point the Queen whispered to him, "It seems that the simplest thing to do would be to ask him how much rice that is."

The wise man was silent for a long time. And then the small wooden chessboard next to the King seemed to catch his interest.

"Very well, sire," the wise man said at last. "I ask only this: Tomorrow, for the first square of your chessboard, give me one grain of rice; the next day, for the second square, two grains of rice; the next day after that, four grains of rice; then, the following day, eight grains for the next square of your chessboard. Thus for each square give me twice the number of grains of the square before it, and so on for every square of the chessboard."

"But *I* wish you to be rewarded," said the King in a stern voice. There was a quiet murmuring among the councillors and nobles assembled in the great hall. The King was getting angry. But the wise man seemed not to notice.

"Truly, sire," the wise man said calmly, "I can think of no way you could reward me—"

"You *shall* choose a reward," said the King, "or I promise, you will wish you had!"

"You have served me well," said the King to the wise man. "What do you wish as a reward?"

The wise man bowed and said, "Serving Your Majesty is reward in itself."

"Indeed, indeed," said the King, "but it must not be said that the King does not reward those who serve him."

"Truly, sire," said the wise man, "I wish no other reward than to serve you again."

Once, long ago, in what is now India, there lived a wise man who performed a service for the King of Deccan. In due course the King summoned the wise man to appear before him.

For my mother, Doris Birch

D. B.

To Yvette, Sivan, Leo, and Alice

D. G.

Published by Dial Books for Young Readers
A Division of NAL Penguin Inc.
2 Park Avenue · New York, New York 10016

Published simultaneously in Canada by Fitzhenry & Whiteside Limited, Toronto
Text copyright © 1988 by David Birch
Pictures copyright © 1988 by Devis Grebu
Printed in Hong Kong by South China Printing Co.
Design by Sara Reynolds
First Edition
W
1 3 5 7 9 10 8 6 4 2

Library of Congress Cataloging in Publication Data

Birch, David, 1942– . The king's chessboard.
Summary: A proud king, too vain to admit what he does not know,
learns a valuable lesson when he readily grants
his wise man a special request.
[1. Pride and vanity—Fiction.]
I. Grebu, Devis, 1933– , ill. II. Title.
PZ7.B511876Ki 1988   [E]   87-20164
ISBN 0-8037-0365-1
ISBN 0-8037-0367-8 (lib. bdg.)

The full-color artwork was prepared using black ink, watercolor,
and colored pencils. It was then color-separated and reproduced
as red, blue, yellow, and black halftones.

The King's Chessboard

David Birch · pictures by Devis Grebu

Dial Books for Young Readers
NEW YORK